The Eternal Truth

Sri Mata Amritanandamayi

Mata Amritanandamayi Center
San Ramon, California, United States

The Eternal Truth
by Sri Mata Amritanandamayi
Compiled by Swami Jnanamritananda Puri
English translation by Dr. M.N. Namboodiri

Published by:
>   Mata Amritanandamayi Center
>   P.O. Box 613
>   San Ramon, CA 94583
>   United States

First printing by MA Center: June 2015

Copyright © 2015 by Mata Amritanandamayi Center, San Ramon, California, USA

All rights reserved No part of this publication may be stored in a retrieval system, transmitted, reproduced, transcribed or translated into any language, in any form, by any means without the prior agreement and written permission of the publisher.

In India:
>   www.amritapuri.org

In USA:
>   www.amma.org

In Europe:
>   www.amma-europe.org

Foreword

"Truth is One. The sages call it by different names." This is the exalted message that the ancient civilization of India has given the world. The cause of all the current problems related to religion is the fact that we have forgotten this message.

We may declare that the world has shrunk to the size of a village thanks to globalization and modern scientific innovations such as the Internet and satellite TV, but, at the same time, the distance between people's minds is steadily increasing. The concept that India has given to the world – *Vasudhaiva kutumbakam*, "The whole world is my family" – is based on the fundamental oneness and actual mental unity of us all. The ultimate solution to our problems is to imbibe this principle of oneness. Even if we are unable to do this, we should at least cultivate the attitude of respecting other people's viewpoints and ideas.

The Eternal Truth

The world is in profound need of tolerance and understanding. The principles of *Sanatana Dharma*, the Eternal Principle, which have been expressed in the words of the *Rishis* (Self-realized sages), are capable of leading us in that direction. These principles are divine beacons shedding light on our path towards perfection.

Sanatana Dharma embodies the eternal truths that everyone, irrespective of religion, caste, or culture, can imbibe and adopt in life.

This book contains the first part of a collection of Amma's answers to questions on the principles of Sanatana Dharma. These questions were raised by devotees on different occasions. We hope that this book will help to promote an understanding of the principles of Sanatana Dharma

The Publishers

Question: What are the special features of Hinduism?

Amma: My children, according to Hinduism, there is Divinity in everything; everyone is an embodiment of God. Humans and God are not two; they are one. Divinity lies latent in every human being. Hinduism teaches that anyone can realize the Divinity within through self effort. The Creator and creation are not separate. The Creator (God) manifests as creation. In Hinduism, to realize this non-dual Truth is considered to be the ultimate goal of life.

The dream is not separate from the dreamer. But we have to wake up in order to see that what we have experienced is a dream. Although everything is God, we perceive everything around us as something separate, because we haven't yet awakened to that awareness. We feel attachment towards some things and aversion towards others. Because of this, happiness and sorrow have become the nature of life.

When we awaken to our true essence, there is no 'I' or 'you' – everything is God. What remains is only bliss. Hinduism teaches that there are many paths that help us awaken to this experience, depending on each one's samskara[1]. There is probably no other religion that has so many different paths, practices, and observances.

We can mold clay in the shape of a donkey, a horse, a mouse, or a lion. Even though they are different in name and form, they are in fact nothing but clay. We need the eye to see the clay that is the substratum of all those names and forms. So, the mode of perceiving the universe through different names and forms has to be abandoned. It is, in fact, the one Supreme Principle that has transformed itself into all those forms. So, in Hinduism everything is God. There is nothing that is not God. Hinduism teaches us to love and serve animals, birds, reptiles, trees, plants, mountains, rivers – everything, even a deadly, poisonous cobra.

When we reach the ultimate experience, we realize that this universe is not distinct from us, just as the different organs in our body are not separate from us.

---

[1] Samskara has two meanings: The totality of impressions imprinted in the mind by experiences from this or previous lives, which influence the life of a human being – his or her nature, actions, state of mind, etc.; the kindling of right understanding (knowledge) within each person, leading to the refinement of his or her character.

Our awareness, which until now has been limited to our body, expands to encompass the entire universe. Nothing is excluded from this awareness. Those who know the Truth experience the suffering and sorrows of others as their own, just as we become aware of pain when our toe is pricked by a thorn. Compassion becomes their true nature, just as heat is the nature of fire, coolness the nature of water, and fragrance and beauty the nature of a flower. Giving solace to others becomes their innate nature. If our finger happens to poke our eye, we forgive our finger and we caress and comfort the eye, because the finger and the eye are not separate from ourselves.

The aim of Hinduism is to take us to the experience that all beings are part of ourselves. When our consciousness expands from limited body-consciousness to include the whole universe, and we experience our oneness with God, then we attain perfection. Sanatana Dharma teaches us the way to see God everywhere in the universe, and thus to experience that we are not separate from God. Different paths are suggested to achieve this, such as the path of selfless action (karma yoga), the path of devotion (bhakti yoga), the path of self-inquiry (jnana yoga), and the path of meditation (raja yoga).

The Hindu religion is called Sanatana Dharma, the Eternal Principle, because it is appropriate for any country during any age. It teaches the eternal truths for the upliftment of all the worlds[2]. Hinduism aims at the upward progress of everyone. In Hinduism there is no room for sectarianism or narrow-mindedness.

Om asato ma satgamaya
tamaso ma jyotirgamaya
mrityor ma amritam gamaya

O Supreme Being,
Lead us from untruth to truth,
From darkness to light,
And from death to immortality.

– Brihadaranyaka Upanishad (1. 3. 28)

Om purnamadah purnamidam
purnat purnamudachyate
purnasya purnamadaya
purnamevavasishyate

---

[2] Heaven, earth, and the netherworld

That is whole, this is whole.
From the whole the whole becomes manifest.
On removing the whole from the whole,
The whole alone remains.[3]

These are mantras the great sages have bequeathed to us, and in these mantras we cannot find even a trace of a viewpoint that sees anyone as 'other' or separate.

The Rishis, India's sages of antiquity, were enlightened seers who had realized the non-dual Supreme Truth. And this Truth flowed into their words, so that they were never untrue.

"God resides even in this pillar," said the boy Prahlada in answer to his father's question. This statement came to be true: God manifested from within that pillar. This is why it is said that truth comes to the words of the sages. Normally, a new birth takes place through the mother's womb – but also the resolve, the mental concept, of a Rishi manifests as a new creation. In other words, what the Rishis say becomes the truth. Each word of

---

[3] If we light a thousand lamps from one lamp, the brightness of that one lamp doesn't diminish. Everything is whole, complete. This famous mantra is the peace invocation in the Upanishads of the Shukla Yajurveda.

those sages, who were fully aware of the past, present, and future, was uttered with the future generations also in mind.

The refrigerator cools, the heater warms, the lamp gives light, the fan provides airflow – but it is the same electric current that makes all of those objects work. Would it be rational to say that the current in one of those objects is superior to the current flowing through the others, just because the instruments have different functions and different monetary values? To understand that the electricity is the same even though the instruments are different, we need to know the science behind those instruments and have some practical experience on the subject. Similarly, the internal essence – the Consciousness – that dwells within each object in the universe is one and the same, even though these objects all appear to be different when viewed externally. Through our spiritual practice, we have to develop the eye of wisdom to see this. The great Rishis, who learned the Truth through their direct experience, passed the Truth on to subsequent generations. It is this philosophy, given to us by the Rishis, that shaped the way of life of the people of India.

'Hindu' is the name that was given to the people who followed this culture in general. It is not really a religion. It is a way of life. The Sanskrit word matham (religion) also has a more general meaning: viewpoint. This particular culture is the sum total of the experiences of many Rishis who lived during different ages and experienced the Ultimate Truth directly. Thus, Sanatana Dharma is not a religion created by a single individual, nor is it a teaching encoded in a single book. It is an all-encompassing philosophy of life.

The great souls living in different countries during different epochs gave their disciples instructions on how to attain God (or the Ultimate Truth). These instructions later became different religions. But that which in India became Sanatana Dharma consists of the everlasting principles, values, and ethical teachings that were revealed to a large number of Self-realized souls as their own experience. Later it came to be known as Hinduism. It is all-encompassing.

Sanatana Dharma doesn't insist that God should be called only by a particular name or that God can be attained only through one prescribed path. Sanatana

Dharma is like a vast supermarket where everything is available. It gives us the freedom to follow any one of the paths indicated by the great Self-realized souls, and even to open up a new path to the goal. There is even the freedom to believe or not to believe in God.

What Sanatana Dharma calls liberation is the ultimate release from human sorrow and suffering. However, there is no insistence on there being only one way to attain this goal. The spiritual master suggests a method that is most conducive to the physical, mental, and intellectual condition of the disciple. All doors cannot be opened with the same key. In a similar way, to open our minds we need different keys to fit our different samskaras and levels of understanding.

How many people will benefit from a river that flows only along a single course? If, instead, the river flows through a number of channels, the people living along the banks of all of those channels will benefit. Similarly, because spiritual masters teach different paths, more people are able to imbibe the teachings. A deaf child has to be taught in sign language. A blind child is taught through Braille, through the sense of touch. And if a child is mentally retarded, we have to go down to his or her level and explain things in a simple, understandable way. Only when the teaching is suited to them can the different students absorb what is being taught. Similarly, spiritual masters examine the mental attitude and samskara of each disciple and decide, accordingly, which path to prescribe for him or her. Regardless of how different the paths are, the goal is always the same: the Ultimate Truth.

In Sanatana Dharma, the garment that is made is not cut to the same measure for everyone. Furthermore, for each individual, the garment may have to be remodeled at times, to fit the person's stage of development.

Spiritual paths and practices have to be renewed according to the times. This is the contribution the great souls have made to Sanatana Dharma. This dynamism and expansiveness are the hallmarks of Hinduism.

If a breast-feeding infant is given meat, he or she won't be able to digest it. The baby will get sick, and this will also be a hardship for others. A diversity of foods is offered depending on the digestive power and tastes of different people. This keeps people healthy. Similarly, in Sanatana Dharma the mode of worship is different for different people according to their samskara. Each individual can choose the method that is best suited for him or her. Whatever path we prefer, whatever path is most conducive to our individual nature, can be found in Sanatana Dharma. This is how numerous spiritual paths, such as jnana yoga, bhakti yoga, karma yoga, raja yoga, hatha yoga, kundalini yoga, kriya yoga, svara yoga, laya yoga, mantra yoga, tantra and nadopasana, came into being.

In Sanatana Dharma there is no contradiction between spirituality and worldly life (living as a householder). Sanatana Dharma doesn't reject worldly life in the name of spirituality. Instead, it teaches that through spirituality your life becomes richer and more meaningful.

The Rishis also built the material sciences and the arts on the foundation of spirituality. They viewed the arts and sciences as steps that lead to the Supreme Truth, and formulated them in a way that will ultimately lead to God. In India, countless scientific disciplines developed in this way – linguistics, architecture, vastu, astronomy, mathematics, the health sciences, diplomacy and economics, natya shastra, musicology, the science of erotica, logic, and nadi shastra, to name a few of these areas. Sanatana Dharma doesn't deny or reject any sphere of human life or culture. The tradition that existed in India was one that encouraged all arts and sciences.

Because it was recognized that the Divine Consciousness exists in all sentient and insentient things, a tradition developed in Sanatana Dharma that everything was to be viewed with respect and reverence. The great Rishis looked upon birds, animals, plants, and trees without a hint of disrespect or aversion, and considered all beings as direct manifestations of God. Thus temples were built even for serpents and birds. Even the spider and the lizard were given a place in temple worship. Sanatana Dharma teaches that a human being needs to earn the blessings even of an ant to achieve perfection. In the Bhagavatam[4] there is a story of an avadhut[5] who adopts twenty-four gurus, including birds and animals. We need to have the attitude of

---

[4] One of eighteen scriptures known as the Puranas, dealing especially with the incarnations of Vishnu, and, in great detail, with the life of Krishna. It emphasizes the path of devotion.

[5] A Self-realized soul who doesn't follow social conventions. By conventional standards, avadhuts are considered extremely eccentric.

always being a beginner, because there are lessons to be learned from all beings.

The Rishis perceived God's presence also in inert objects. They sang, Sarvam brahmamayam, re re sarvam brahmamayam – "All is Brahman; all is the essence of the Supreme." Nowadays scientists say that everything consists of energy. The people of India who believe in the words of the Rishis bow down to everything with devotion, seeing everything as God.

Amma[6] remembers certain things from her childhood. If she happened to step on a piece of paper that had been swept into the garbage, she would touch it and bow down to it. If she didn't do this, she'd receive a spanking from her mother. Amma's mother used to tell her that that paper wasn't just a mere piece of paper; it was Goddess Saraswati, the Goddess of Learning, Herself.

In a similar way, Amma was taught that if she accidentally stepped on cow dung, she should touch it as a sign of her reverence. Cow dung helps the grass to grow. The cows eat grass and give us milk. We use that milk.

---

[6] Amma usually refers to herself in the third person as "Amma" (Mother).

Amma's mother taught her that we shouldn't touch a doorsill with our foot. If we happen to step on it, we should touch it with our hand and bow to it. The reason for this is probably that, symbolically, the doorway is the entrance leading to the next stage in life. When you look at things in this way, everything becomes precious. Nothing can then be ignored or disrespected. So, we should look upon everything with respect and reverence.[7]

The Bhagavatam (the story of the Lord) and Bhagavan (the Lord) are not two; they are the same. The world and God are not two. We thus see unity in diversity, in the manifold. Because of this, even now when Amma happens to step on something, she touches it and then touches her head to show her reverence towards that object. Even though she knows that God isn't separate from her, Amma still bows down to everything. Even though the staircase, which helps us get to the upper floor, and the upper floor itself are built out of the same

---

[7] Some people may wonder why Amma gives such importance to everything in the manifested world, which, according to Sanatana Dharma, is maya (illusion). Referring to this, Amma says: "When we say that the external world is not true or real, but untrue or illusory, we do not mean that it doesn't exist, but that it isn't permanent, that it is constantly in a state of change."

material, Amma cannot ignore the staircase. She cannot forget the path that has been followed to reach there. Amma respects all observances that help us to reach the ultimate goal.

Her children may ask whether Amma needs to have this attitude. But let us say that a child has jaundice and cannot eat salt because it will worsen his condition. The child doesn't like food without salt, so if he sees anything with salt in it, he'll grab it and eat it. His mother doesn't add any salt to the dishes she prepares, and for the sake of that child, the other healthy family members also avoid eating salt. Similarly, Amma is setting an example even though she doesn't need to follow any of those customs.

Because Sanatana Dharma teaches us to see Divinity in everything, there is no such thing as eternal hell. It is believed that no matter how great a sin you have committed, you can still purify yourself through good thoughts and deeds and finally realize God. With sincere remorse, anyone can escape from the effects of his or her mistakes, regardless of the gravity of those mistakes. There is no sin that cannot be washed away with repentance. But this shouldn't be like the bath of an elephant! The elephant bathes and emerges out of the water, only to pour dust all over itself again without delay. This is how many people behave with their mistakes.

We may make many mistakes as we proceed through life. But Amma's children shouldn't be discouraged because of this. If you fall, think only that you have fallen in order to get up. Don't just lie there thinking that it's quite comfortable! And don't feel shattered by the fall. You have to make an attempt to get up and go forward.

When we write on a piece of paper with a pencil, we can use an eraser if we make a mistake, and rewrite our words. But if we again and again make a mistake in the same place and try to erase it, the paper may get torn. So, my children, try not to repeat your mistakes. To make mistakes is natural, but try to be careful. Be alert!

Sanatana Dharma doesn't reject anyone as unworthy forever. To consider someone unworthy of the spiritual path is like deciding, after building a hospital, that no patients are allowed. Even a broken watch will show the correct time twice a day! So, what is needed is acceptance. When we avoid someone as 'unsuitable,' we are helping to engender vengefulness and animal instincts in that person, and he or she will again slip into error. On the other hand, if we praise what is good in such people and try patiently to correct their mistakes, we can uplift them.

We make mistakes because we are ignorant about who we really are. Sanatana Dharma doesn't reject anyone; its teachings provide everyone with the knowledge that is needed. If the sages had labeled the hunter Ratnakara as nothing but a robber and had kept him away, the sage Valmiki would not have been born[8]. Sanatana Dharma shows that even a robber can be transformed into a great soul.

No one will reject a diamond even if it lies in excreta. Someone will pick it up, clean it, and make it their own. It isn't possible to reject anyone since the Supreme Being is present in everyone. We should be able to see God in everyone, regardless of a person's stature in society, whether it be high or low. For this to be possible, we first have to wash away the impurities that cover our own minds.

The teachings of Sanatana Dharma are imperishable gems that the selfless Rishis, out of their compassion, have given the world. Anyone wishing to stay alive cannot avoid air or water. Similarly,

---

[8] See the story of Valmiki in the glossary.

anyone seeking peace cannot ignore the principles of Sanatana Dharma. Sanatana Dharma doesn't ask us to believe in a God who lives up in the sky. It says, "Have faith in yourself. Everything is within you!"

An atom bomb has the power to reduce a continent to ashes, but its strength lies in the tiny atoms. A banyan tree can cover a wide area, and yet it grows out of a small seed. The point is that the essence of God exists within each of us. We can learn this through reason and through the experiences we have in our spiritual practice. All we need to do is to carefully follow one of the methods of awakening this power.

Devotion, faith, and attentive awareness in every action – this is what Sanatana Dharma teaches. It doesn't ask you to blindly believe in anything. If we want to use a machine, we first have to learn how to operate it, otherwise it could get damaged. Knowledge (jnana) is required to perform our actions in the right way. Performing our actions with the awareness that comes from understanding that knowledge – that is attentive awareness.

A man pours water into a water tank. But even after having done this the whole day, the tank still isn't full. He tries to find out why. Finally, he discovers that one of the outlet holes in the tank hasn't been plugged. Here, the knowledge is the understanding that without plugging the hole, no amount of water will be enough to fill the tank. Attentive awareness is what we apply to effort after acquiring that knowledge. Only when we perform actions with attentive awareness will we obtain the intended result.

Five farm workers were given the job of planting seeds. One of them dug holes in the earth. Another put fertilizer in the holes. A third watered the ground. Another man covered the holes with soil. Days went by, but none of the seeds sprouted. The farmer examined the soil to find out what was wrong, and discovered that the worker entrusted with putting the seeds in the holes hadn't done his job! So, this is what action without attentive awareness is like; it won't yield the desired result.

The aim of every action we perform in life is to bring us closer to God. We should perform our actions selflessly, without the feeling of 'I.' We should understand that we are able to act only because of God's grace and power. This is knowledge (jnana) in the context of action (karma). An action performed with such knowledge and attentive awareness is karma yoga, the yoga of selfless action.

When we practice attentive awareness while performing an action, we forget ourselves. The mind becomes one-pointed. We experience bliss. This is how devotion is born. When we make an effort with attentive awareness and devotion, our effort will surely bear fruit. And when we get the fruit of that action, our faith becomes firm. Such faith is unwavering. No one can shake that faith. Attentive awareness, devotion, and faith: actions done with attentive awareness cultivate devotion, and this leads to faith.

Most of the texts of Sanatana Dharma are written in the form of discussions. They contain the Self-realized master's answers to the disciple's questions. The disciple has the freedom to ask any questions until his or her doubts are completely cleared. This develops attentive awareness in the disciple.

Hinduism isn't against anyone. Nor does it require anyone to give up his or her religion or faith. In fact, it considers it an unrighteous act to destroy someone's faith. According to Sanatana Dharma, all religions are different pathways to the same goal. It doesn't negate anything. Everything is included. For a Hindu there is no such thing as a separate religion. Originally, such a concept didn't exist in India.

Whatever religion a person belongs to, he or she should remain steadfast in faith and go forward in life. Only this will help the seeker to reach the ultimate goal. The paths of karma yoga, bhakti yoga, and jnana yoga can all be followed by people of any religious faith in a manner suited to the present age and its lifestyles.

The ocean and its waves can be a nightmare for those who do not know how to swim. On the other hand, those who know how to swim will revel among the ocean waves. Similarly, for those who have imbibed the principles of spirituality, life is blissful. For them, life is a festival. What we need is a way to experience bliss during this life itself, not after death. Just as one has to learn the art of business management to be successful in business, it is essential to learn the art of life management in order to be truly happy in life. Sanatana Dharma is the comprehensive science of life management.

The contents of the Indian scriptures, such as the Upanishads, Bhagavad Gita, Brahma Sutras,

Ramayana, and Mahabharata, are all eternal truths that people of all ages can grasp. These texts are not sectarian; they are works based on reason and can be put into practice by anyone. The texts on Sanatana Dharma can be understood by everyone, just like texts on health, psychology, and social science. Imbibing the principles of Sanatana Dharma will lead to happiness and the upliftment of all humanity.

Question: Why do we need to believe in God?

Amma: It is possible to go through life without believing in a Supreme Being. But to be able to go forward with firm, unfaltering steps when faced with a crisis, we need to take refuge in God. We should be ready to follow God's path.

A life without God is like a court case in which two lawyers are arguing without a judge being present. The hearing will go nowhere. If they proceed without the judge, no ruling is possible.

The Eternal Truth

We worship God so that the divine qualities within us can be nurtured. But there is actually no need for faith if you can imbibe those qualities without it. Whether we believe or not, the Supreme Being exists as the Truth, and whether we recognize that Truth or not, it cannot be diminished in any way.

The earth's gravitational force is a fact; it won't cease to exist just because we don't believe in it. If we deny the existence of gravity and jump from a height, we will have to accept the truth through the adverse effect we receive from the fall. Turning away from a reality like that is like creating darkness by closing one's eyes. By recognizing the Universal Truth that is God, and living in accordance with that Truth, we can have a trouble-free passage through life.

Question: What is the principle behind worshipping an image?

Amma: Hindus do not actually worship the images themselves. They worship the Supreme Power that pervades each image. When a little boy sees a painting of his father, he thinks of his father and not of the artist who painted it. When a young man sees a pen or a handkerchief given by his beloved, he thinks about her, not about the object. He won't get rid of it for anything in the world. To him, that pen is no ordinary pen; that handkerchief is not a mere handkerchief. In those objects he feels the woman he loves.

If an ordinary object can generate such powerful feelings in a man or a woman in love, think of how valuable a divine image will be to a devotee if it reminds that person of God! To the devotee, the sculpted image of the Supreme Being is not a mere piece of rock; it is an embodiment of the Supreme Consciousness.

Some people ask, "Isn't marriage the mere tying of a knot?" Yes, that's true; it's just the tying of an ordinary string[9] around the neck. But think of how much value we attach to that piece of string

---

[9] In a traditional Hindu wedding ceremony, a string or a chain with a pendant is tied around the bride's neck. This is worn throughout her married life and symbolizes the lasting bond between the husband and wife.

and to that moment! It is a moment that lays the foundation for life. The value of that ceremony has nothing to do with the value of the string, but with the total value of life itself. In the same way, the value of a divine image doesn't lie in the value of the stone. That image is priceless, its place equal to the Universal Father/Mother. Anyone who sees the image as just a piece of rock does so out of ignorance. A ritual worship normally begins with the resolve, "I worship God in this image."

It would be difficult for ordinary individuals to worship the all-pervading Supreme Consciousness without the help of some sort of symbol to represent it. An image of the Divine can be very helpful in nurturing devotion and in making the mind one-pointed. As we stand before the image, we pray with our eyes closed. Thus the image helps us to focus our minds inward and to awaken the divine essence within us.

There is another important principle behind this kind of worship. Gold bangles, earrings, necklaces, and rings are all made of the same metal. Their substance is gold. Similarly, God is the substratum of everything. We should be able to perceive the underlying unity in diversity. Whether it be Shiva,

Vishnu, or Muruga (Subramanya)[10], we should be aware of the oneness behind them. We need to understand that all the different forms are different manifestations of one God. Different forms are adopted because people belong to different cultures. So, everyone can select the form that he or she prefers.

We have to remove the dirt and dust from the mirror before we can clearly see our faces in it. Similarly, only when we remove the impurities that have settled in our minds can we see God. Our ancestors established image worship and other practices as a part of Sanatana Dharma to purify our minds and make our minds one-pointed. In Sanatana Dharma, we seek God within ourselves, not somewhere out there. When we experience God within us, we are able to see God everywhere.

God has no inside or outside. God is the Divine Consciousness that exists everywhere, pervading everything. It is only because we have individual identities, the feeling of 'I,' that there is a perception of 'within' and 'without.' At present, our minds are turned outwards, not within. The mind is attached

---

[10] Muruga is a god created by Shiva to assist souls in their evolution, especially through the practice of yoga. He is the brother of Ganesha.

to many different things outside of ourselves and to the notion of 'mine' in relation to those things. The aim of image worship is to bring the mind back within and to awaken the Divine Consciousness which is already present within us.

Question: Some people criticize the Hindu faith because of its practice of image worship. Is there any real basis for this?

Amma: It is not clear why anyone would want to criticize this. Image worship can be found in all religions in one form or another – in Christianity, Islam, Buddhism, etc. The only difference is in the image that is worshipped and in the way the worship is performed. In Christianity, sweet dishes or flower petals are not offered; they light candles instead. The Christian priest offers the bread as Christ's body and the wine as his blood. And while Hindus worship with burning camphor, many Christians burn incense. Christians also see the cross as a symbol of sacrifice and selflessness. They kneel before the form of Christ and pray.

In Islam, people view Mecca as sacred and prostrate in that direction. They sit in front of the Kabaa, praying and contemplating God's qualities. All these prayers are meant to awaken the positive qualities that are present within us.

We first learn the simple consonants, ka, kha, ga, gha in Malayalam, so that later we can learn to read words with composite sounds; and we begin with a, b, and c to learn to read English. Similarly, all the different forms of worship lead to the development of godly qualities within us.

Question: Regarding image worship, shouldn't we worship the sculptor who made the divine form rather than the sculpture itself?

Amma: When you see the flag of your country, is it the flag or the tailor you respect? Or perhaps the weaver who wove the fabric? Or the person who spun the yarn? Or the farmer who grew the cotton? No one gives a thought to those people. Instead, we are reminded of the country that the flag symbolizes.

In the same way, when we see a divine image, it is not the sculptor who comes to mind; it is God, the Divine Sculptor of the entire universe, whom we remember. The Supreme Being is the Source from which the artist gets the inspiration and the strength to chisel the image. If we can agree that there has to be a sculptor to make an image, why, then, is it so hard to believe that this universe may also have been created by a Sculptor?

By worshipping a divine image, we develop the expansiveness of heart needed to love and respect every living being, including the sculptor of that image. By praying to and visualizing God within the image, we are purified within and raised to the level where we see and worship God in everything. This is the aim of image worship. While all the symbols that remind us of the material world ultimately limit and confine us, the symbols that awaken our awareness of the Divine lead us to a state of expansiveness way beyond all limits. Image worship helps us to see God everywhere, in everything.

Question: Where did image worship originate?

Amma: In the Satya Yuga, the Age of Truth[11], Prahlada, the young son of the demon king Hiranyakashipu, declared, "God exists even in this pillar!" in response to a question put to him by his father. God then emerged out of that pillar in the form of Narasimha, the Divine Man-lion. Since the all-pervading God thus appeared out of a pillar, making Prahlada's resolve come true, we can say that this was the first instance of image worship.

Prahlada's story is famous. The demon king Hiranyakashipu wanted to subdue all three worlds and make sure he would never die. So he performed severe austerities aimed at pleasing Lord Brahma, the Creator. Brahma was pleased with his austerities. He appeared before Hiranyakashipu and offered him a boon. The demon king said, "The boon I want is that I am not to be killed by anything in your creation. I am not to meet with death on a shore or in water, in the sky or on earth. I am not to die in a

---

[11] The Satya Yuga is referred to as the Golden Age. There are four yugas (ages or aeons). See glossary.

room or outside. I am not to die during the day or at night, and not be killed by a man or a woman, by celestial beings (devas) or demons (asuras), or any vertebrates, neither human nor animal. Nor am I to be killed by any weapon." Brahma blessed him, saying, "So be it!" and disappeared.

But something else happened while the king was performing his austerities. In his absence, the celestial beings defeated the demons in battle. Indra, the king of the celestial beings, captured Hiranyakashipu's pregnant wife, Kayadhu, and carried her away. On the way, he encountered the sage Narada. On Narada's advice, Indra left Kayadhu in the sage's hermitage and returned to the celestial world. During the time Kayadhu stayed with Narada, the sage taught her the essence of the Bhagavatam, and the infant in her womb heard his discourses.

Having completed his austerities, Hiranyakashipu returned and defeated the devas in a battle. He then went to the sage's hermitage and brought his wife back to his palace. The strength of the boon he had been given earlier boosted his ego. He conquered all three worlds. He made the devas his servants. He harassed the sages and worshippers and destroyed their yaga yajnas, elaborate Vedic sacrificial rites. He declared that no one was allowed to chant any mantra other than Hiranyaya Namah (Salutations to Hiranya, i.e., himself).

In time, his wife gave birth to a son. The child was given the name Prahlada. Because he remembered all the teachings given by Narada, he grew up as a devotee of Lord Vishnu. When the time came for Prahlada to begin his studies, his father sent him to a gurukula[12]. After some time, the king became anxious to find out what his son had learned, so he called Prahlada back to the palace. As soon as Prahlada arrived, his father asked him what he had learned. Prahlada said, "Lord Vishnu should be worshipped through the nine methods: hearing His stories, singing His glories, remembering Him, serving at His feet, worshipping Him, saluting Him, being His servant, being His friend, and surrendering oneself completely to Him." The boy hadn't learned this at school; he had heard it while still in his mother's womb. When Hiranyakashipu heard his son say that Vishnu, Hiranyakashipu's enemy, should be worshipped, he became so enraged that

---

[12] An ashram with a living guru, where disciples live and study with the guru. In the olden days, the gurukulas were boarding schools where youngsters were given a comprehensive education based on the Vedas.

he ordered his soldiers to kill his son. The soldiers tried to kill the boy in several different ways, but failed. Hiranyakashipu finally gave up and sent his son back to the gurukula to wipe out the devotion in him. But, instead, the other asura children at the school who happened to hear Prahlada's advice also became devotees of the Lord. When Hiranyakashipu was told about this he again became enraged and asked his son, "If there is a God of the three worlds other than myself, where is He?" "God is everywhere," Prahlada replied. "Is He in this pillar?" roared Hiranyakashipu. "Yes, He resides in the pillar as well," said Prahlada. Hiranyakashipu responded by hitting the pillar forcefully with his fist. The pillar split in two and from within it the ferocious Narasimha, the Divine Man-lion, emerged. This happened during twilight. The Lord sat down on the threshold of the palace, placed the demon king on His lap and killed him by tearing open his chest using nothing but His fingernails.

Thus, the words that came from the innocent heart of Prahlada came true. This was the beginning of image worship. His faith was so strong that he believed God existed even in a pillar, and so firm was his conviction that what he believed became an actual experience. We should look at the principle behind this story. God Almighty can take any form. God can have attributes or be attributeless. Saltwater can become salt crystals, and salt crystals can become saltwater.

This story also reveals another principle: the limitations of the human being. The intelligence of God is beyond the grasp of the most intelligent and powerful person on earth. There is a limit to how far human intelligence can reach, but God's intelligence is boundless.

Hiranyakashipu had asked for his boon very carefully, with the intention of avoiding death forever. When he received that boon, he firmly believed no one could possibly defeat him. But he did not know God. God has a solution for everything.

Neither day nor night. Solution: twilight. Not in water nor on land: God put the demon king on His lap. Neither outside, nor inside: He sat on the doorstep. Neither man nor animal: He took the form of a Man-lion. No weapon was used: He killed the king with His fingernails. Thus, God, in the form of Narasimha, slew the unrighteous

Hiranyakashipu without violating any of the boons given by Brahma.

God is beyond the reach of human intelligence. There is only one way to know God: by offering oneself fully and taking refuge at His[13] feet – the way of complete surrender.

Humans have the intelligence of the ego and the power of discrimination. Discrimination (viveka) is pure intelligence; it has no impurities. It is like a mirror. God is clearly reflected in it. But only those who surrender to God can break through the limitations of their human intelligence and go beyond it.

Some people say, "Can you see God with your eyes? I don't believe in what I cannot see!" But a human being is limited in every way. Our senses of sight and hearing are very limited. People don't think about this.

Amma has a question. You can't see the current in a live wire. Do you say there is no current, just because you cannot see it? You'll get a shock if you touch it. That is experience.

Suppose you set a bird free to fly away. It flies higher and higher, until it finally soars to such a

---

[13] Amma has said that God is beyond any definition of gender. However, when Amma talks, she refers to God in the more traditional way, using the word 'He.'

height that it can no longer be seen. Do we say that the bird no longer exists because we cannot see it? What logic is there in deciding we will believe only in that which falls within the limited range of our eyesight?

For a judge, the statements of a thousand people who say they didn't see a crime being committed do not prove a thing. The proof lies with the one person who says he or she witnessed the crime. Similarly, whoever says there is no God doesn't prove anything; the proof lies in the words of the holy sages who have experienced God.

An atheist went around arguing that there is no God. He came to the house of a friend. Inside the house there was a beautiful globe. "Oh, how beautiful it is!" he exclaimed. "Who made it?" His friend, who happened to be a believer, said, "If this artificial model of the earth couldn't have been created without a creator, surely the creation of the real earth requires a Creator!"

It is said that the seed contains a tree. If you pick up a seed and look at it or bite into it, you won't see the tree. But try planting it. Put in some effort. Then a sapling will emerge out of it. It's useless to just talk about it; we have to make an effort. Only then will we reap the experience.

Scientists have faith in the experiments they launch. They may fail in many of their attempts, but they don't give up. They continues with their experiments in the hope of succeeding in their next attempt.

Think of how many years it takes to become a doctor or an engineer. The students don't complain that it's impossible to wait for so long. It is only because they continue their studies with an attitude of surrender that they succeed in reaching their goal.

God isn't someone we can see with our eyes. God is the cause of everything. If you are asked what came first, the mango seed or mango tree, what will you answer? For the tree to be born a seed is required, and for the seed to exist there first has to be a tree. So, there is a separate cause behind the tree and the seed. That is God. God is the root cause of everything, the Creator of all. God is everything. The way to know God is to cultivate the divine qualities within us and to surrender our egos to God. Then godliness will become our experience.

Prahlada exemplifies the most exalted type of devotion. It would be difficult to find a devotee with as much surrender as Prahlada. When we fail to succeed in what we set out to achieve, we usually blame someone else and retreat. Furthermore, when difficulties arise in life, our faith usually crumbles. We blame God. But look at Prahlada. His father's soldiers tried to kill him by pushing him under water; they threw him into boiling oil; they threw him down a mountain; they set him on fire. They tried again and again to kill him. But on each of those occasions, Prahlada's faith didn't falter even a little. Because of his unshakable faith, no harm came to him. When his life was being threatened, he kept repeating the mantra, "Narayana! Narayana!" He was also told many things intended to destroy his faith in God: "Sri Hari (Vishnu) is not God! He is a thief! There's no such thing as God!" and so on. Even then, Prahlada kept repeating the divine name with attentive awareness.

In most cases, the moment we hear something negative about someone, our trust in that person is lost. If some suffering comes our way, we lose our faith. Our devotion is just part-time devotion. We call out to God when we need something;

otherwise, we don't remember God at all. And if our desires are not fulfilled, our faith disappears. This is our condition. But despite the difficulties Prahlada had to go through, he never faltered. His faith became stronger with each crisis. The more obstacles that appeared, the more firmly he held on to God's feet. This is how complete his surrender to God was. As a result, Prahlada became a beacon giving light to the entire world. Even today, his story and his devotion spread light into the hearts of thousands.

Prahlada is distinguished by his devotion and his realization of non-duality (advaita). Whatever a person of total surrender like Prahlada touches will 'turn to gold.' This is the state of the attitude of self-surrender.

Prahlada's devotion also led to the liberation of his father, Hiranyakashipu, for to die at the hands of God is to attain liberation. This means that Hiranyakashipu's identification with the body was removed, and he was given the awareness of his true Self (atman). The body doesn't last forever. Hiranyakashipu was made to understand, through his own experience, that only the Self is everlasting.

Human beings are truly miniscule. Yet they take pride in their intelligence and abilities, and they criticize God. God is the Principle beyond all possible human intelligence. The way to reach God is through spiritual practices as prescribed by the Rishis, and one such practice can be worship of the divine images.

Question: In Hinduism, 300 million deities are worshipped. Is there really more than one God?

Amma: In Hinduism there is only one God. Not only does Hinduism teach that there is one Supreme Being, it also declares that there is nothing in the universe other than that Supreme Being. God manifests as everything in the universe. God is the Consciousness that pervades everything. He is beyond all names and forms. But He can also take any form to bless a devotee. He can manifest in any number of different forms and divine moods or states. The wind can appear as a gentle breeze, a strong wind, or a raging storm. What manifestation is impossible for God Almighty, who controls even the storm? Who can describe His glory? Just as air can be still or blow as the wind, and water can turn into steam or ice, God can assume either an attributeless state or a state with attributes. In the same way, it is one and the same God whom Hindus worship in many different forms and states, such as Shiva, Vishnu, Ganesha, Muruga, Durga, Saraswati, and Kali.

Tastes differ from person to person. Individuals grow up in different environments and cultures. In Sanatana Dharma, people have the freedom to worship God in any form or state that suits their own tastes and mental development. This is how the different manifestations of God appear in Hinduism. They are not different Gods. They are all aspects of the one Supreme Being.

Question: If God is omnipresent, what is the need for temples?

Amma: One special characteristic of Sanatana Dharma is that it comes down to the level of each individual and elevates him or her. People have different samskaras. Each individual has to be guided according to his or her inner tendencies. Some patients are allergic to certain injections and have to be given alternative medicines. Similarly, the unique mental and physical characteristics of each person have to be taken into account, and the appropriate methods that suit the samskara of the individual should be prescribed. This is how different traditions are created. The path of devotion, the path of selfless action, worshipping the Divine with attributes and without attributes – all of these paths developed in this way. But they share the same foundation, and that is the discrimination between the eternal and the ephemeral.

The aim of archana[14], devotional singing, and ritual worship is the same. A blind child is taught the alphabet through touch and a deaf child is taught in sign language. Everyone has to be guided according to his or her own level of understanding. Temples are necessary to uplift ordinary people by

---

[14] A form of worship in which the names of a deity are chanted, usually 108, 300, or 1000 names in one sitting.

bringing the Divine down to a physical level. We cannot ignore or reject anyone.

Even though the air is everywhere, we experience it more tangibly next to a fan, don't we? Under a tree there is a special coolness that isn't felt elsewhere; you feel the presence of the wind and experience that coolness. Similarly, when we worship God through an instrument (upadi) that symbolizes Him, His divine presence can be felt more clearly. Even though the sun shines everywhere, in a room where the curtains or shutters are closed we need to switch on a lamp to get light. A cow is full of milk, but we cannot get milk from its ears, only from its udders. God is all-pervading, but His presence can be felt more easily by those who have faith in the temple. But for this to happen, faith is essential. Faith tunes the mind. Even though God is present in the temple, those who lack faith won't experience that presence. It is faith that gives us the experience.

Amma and a few of her Indian children were once watching a dance being performed by western couples. One of Amma's daughters[15] was upset

---

[15] Mother always refers to her disciples and devotees as her children or her sons and daughters.

because the couples were holding hands as they danced. "Oh, no! What kind of dance is that?" she exclaimed. "A man and a woman dancing so close together!" Amma asked her, "If Shiva and Parvati were to dance that closely together, would you feel offended?" We would see the Divinity in that dance, and we wouldn't have a problem with it. When we talk about Shiva and Parvati, there is holiness, there is faith. So that dance would be exalted. On the other hand, because we are unable to see the Divinity in this particular man and woman, we are upset by their behavior! So, the mind is the important factor here. If we stay firmly committed to what we really believe, we can experience God. Faith is the foundation.

Houses of worship, where countless people pray with the same focus of mind, have a unique quality about them, which is not found in other places. A bar or a liquor store doesn't have the same ambience as an office. The atmosphere in a temple is not the same as that of a bar. In the bar you lose your mental health; in the temple you gain it. Places of worship are permeated with the vibrations of positive thoughts. This helps a conflicted mind to regain the feeling of peace and calmness. The air in a perfume factory is special, filled with a wonderful fragrance, while the atmosphere in a chemical factory is entirely different. The devotion-filled atmosphere and the sacred vibrations in the temple help us to concentrate our minds and to awaken love and devotion within ourselves. A temple is like a mirror. In the mirror, we can clearly see the dirt on our faces, which helps us to clean our faces. Similarly, worshipping in a temple helps us to purify our hearts.

Temple worship is the first stage of worshipping God. The temple and the image that is installed there allow us to worship God in a personal way, and to establish a bond with God. But, gradually, we need to develop the ability to see the Divine Consciousness everywhere. This becomes possible when temple worship is done in the proper way. This is the real goal of temple worship.

We show pictures of different types of birds to children and say, "This is a parrot, this is a mynah bird." When the children are older, they no longer need the pictures to identify the birds. Only in the beginning were the pictures necessary.

In truth, everything is God. There is nothing to be excluded.

The stairway and the upper floor of a house are built with the same bricks and cement, but this becomes clear only when one gets to the top. And we need the steps to get there. This illustrates the benefit we get from the temple.

It is often said that you may be born in a temple, but you shouldn't die there. We can make the temple our instrument in our search for God, but we shouldn't be attached to it. Only the release from all attachments will make us fully free. We shouldn't think that God exists only in the temple images. Everything is filled with consciousness, the Supreme Consciousness. Nothing is inert. Through worship we attain the mental disposition to perceive everything as the essence of God, and to love and to serve everything. This is the attitude of profound acceptance towards all. We need to realize that we ourselves and everything around us are God. We should develop the attitude of seeing everything as one, of seeing everything as we see ourselves. What can we possibly hate when we see everything as God? The temple and its rituals are meant to guide us to this state.

The ocean and the waves appear to be different, but both are water. Bracelets, necklaces, rings, and anklets appear to be different and are worn on different parts of the body, but in reality they are all gold. From the perspective of gold, they are all the same; there is no difference. Only when we look at them from an external point of view are they different. In the same way, objects around us may appear to be different, but, in reality, they are all the same. They are Brahman, the Absolute Reality. There is only That. The goal of human life is to realize this, to experience it. Once you experience this realization, your problems vanish completely, just as darkness disappears when the sun rises.

Today, scientists say that everything is energy. The Rishis went one step further and declared that everything is consciousness, the Supreme Consciousness. Sarvam brahmamayam – "All is Brahman, the Supreme Self" – this was the Rishis own experience.

But to realize this, we have to transcend the notion that God resides only in the temple images. We should to be able to see the Supreme in everything. In order to achieve this, temple worship has to be done with the understanding of this principle. It is actually the Self residing within us that we worship. Since this is difficult for most people to understand, we project that Supreme Principle onto the image, like a mirror, and worship it there. While worshipping in the temple, we should construct a temple within ourselves. Then we can see God everywhere. So, this is the aim of worshipping in the temple. It is, in fact, what we are doing when we stand before the inner sanctum, catch a glimpse of the image, and then close our eyes. We see within us the image of God we just saw externally in the inner sanctum of the temple, and then we hope to open our eyes and see God in everything. In this way, we can transcend all forms and realize the all-pervading Self.

For many of us, worshipping God is a part-time activity. What we need is full-time devotion. To pray for the fulfillment of a particular desire is part-time devotion. What we need is the love and devotion for God that leads to Supreme Love. Our only wish should be to love God. That is all we should pray for. We should always focus on God. We should see God in everything. It is God who has given us the power to pray. If God's power were absent, we wouldn't even be able to lift a finger. Full-time devotion is to be constantly aware that it is God who makes us do everything. In this way, we can discard the sense of 'I,' which is rooted in the body-mind-intellect plane, and experience ourselves as the all-pervading Consciousness.

The great poet Kalidasa entered the sacred shrine and closed the door. The Divine Mother came and knocked on the door. When the door failed to open She asked: "Who is inside?" Immediately came the reply: "Who is outside?" Again She said: "Who is inside?" and the same reply was given: "Who is outside?" Finally, the Divine Mother answered: "Kali outside!" And the reply came: "Dasa (servant) inside!"

Although he was repeatedly questioned, he didn't reveal who was inside; he never said his name. Only after he was told, "Kali outside," did he say, "Servant inside!" At that moment, he received a full vision of Kali. When we lose the 'I,' all that remains is 'Thou, God.' The insignificant identity 'I' must be discarded. True devotion is the awareness, "You are all! You make us do everything!" In this way we attain everything, after which there is nothing more to be gained.

God has given us our eyesight. God doesn't need the light of the oil lamp we have spent ten rupees to light! God has nothing to gain from us. When we take refuge in God, we are the ones who gain from it. The money we offer at the temple symbolizes our surrender; it helps us to cultivate the attitude of surrender. Furthermore, when we light a lamp with oil or clarified butter, the atmosphere is purified by the smoke from the flame. We shouldn't make an offering just to make a wish come true. We shouldn't look upon God as someone who takes bribes!

Even the best variety of seeds will fail to sprout if they remain in our hands. We have to let go of the seeds and plant them in the soil. Only with surrender do we reap the benefit. Similarly, the attitude, "This is mine," or "My wish must be fulfilled," has to be abandoned. We need to develop the attitude, "Everything is Yours alone. Let Your will be done!" Only with such surrender will our devotion be complete.

Many people think surrender means that only by giving God something will we get any result. But that is not how surrender should be understood. At present we are still on the level of mind and intellect. "I am this body. I am the son or daughter of so and so. My name is such and such." Those attributes that we have added to the 'I' have to be discarded.

The ego is the only thing we ourselves have created, and that is what has to be renounced. We have to surrender the ego to God. When we surrender the ego, only that which God has created remains. We then become a flute at His lips, or the sound of His conch. To rise to the level of expansiveness, all we need to do is get rid of the individual mind, which is our own creation. Once 'I' and 'mine' are given up, there is no limited individual; there is only That which pervades everything.

A seed won't germinate if it is thrown on a rock. It has to be planted in the soil. In a similar way, if we want to reap the real benefits of our actions and efforts, we have to get rid of our ego. We should cultivate the attitude of surrender. Then, with God's grace, anything can happen.

It is our minds that we should surrender to God. But we cannot just pull out the mind and offer it. So, we offer things that the mind is attached to, and that is the equivalent of surrendering the mind. Some people are fond of payasam (a sweet rice dish), so payasam is offered to God. And when later the payasam is distributed as prasad (a consecrated blessing) to poor children, it serves another purpose. The mind is most strongly attached to wealth. It is to be released from that bond that we offer money in the temple. We also offer flowers at the temple. But what we really should offer to God are the flowers of our hearts. To offer our hearts is true surrender, true devotion. This is what offering flowers symbolizes.

Instead of just demanding, "Give me this and that!" we should also yearn for God's divine qualities like love, compassion, and inner peace. Repeat a mantra, do good deeds, and pray for God's grace. God will give you everything you need. There is no need to ask for anything specific.

Worship God with love. God is aware of all the desires of our minds. Do not think that God will know everything only if we tell Him. You have to tell everything to a lawyer or a doctor, so that the lawyer can argue your case effectively or so the doctor can make the right diagnosis and give you the proper treatment. But God knows everything even if we don't tell Him anything. God is all-knowing. Still, when our hearts are heavy, there's nothing wrong with opening our hearts to God, unloading our burdens before Him. But we have to understand that this is just the beginning. Gradually, we have to learn to worship God selflessly, with no expectations. Then, when we pray for ourselves, we will be praying only for love and devotion towards God. When the only objective of our devotion is to be filled with ever more love and devotion, we will also be given everything else we need. We will benefit materially as well as being spiritually uplifted and developing on the spiritual path. Only through innocent supreme love and devotion can we realize God. We should pray to become one with God. Then His grace will flow to us automatically and we will be filled with divine qualities.

In the temple, try to keep the mind completely focused on God. Circumambulation should be done while repeating a mantra. While standing in front of the shrine for darshan[16],6 close your eyes and visualize the divine form with concentration and meditate on it.

However, it is not enough to just go to the temple and perform a little worship. We should also set aside some time daily for meditation on God. Chant your mantra as much as possible. We acquire spiritual power through this. If we bring together

---

[16] An audience with or a vision of the Divine or a holy person.

the water flowing through different branches of a river and make it flow along a single course, it will become a great power. We can even get electricity from it. In a similar way, the power of the mind is wasted through a multitude of thoughts, but if we focus the mind on just one thought, the mind will become a great power. If the average person is like an ordinary post along an electric power line, a person who performs spiritual austerities is like a power transformer.

We need to understand the basic principles behind worship. Instead of thinking that there are numerous different deities, we should see them all as different forms of the same God.

Today, an increasing number of people are coming to temples. But it is doubtful that the spiritual culture and understanding of people is really developing at the same rate. This is because there is virtually no system in place in the temples to explain our cultural heritage. As a result, people look upon the temple as a means to get their wishes fulfilled. Nowadays when temple-goers close their eyes in prayer, it is their desires that they picture clearly in their minds. Amma doesn't mean you shouldn't have any desires, but when the mind is filled with desires, you cannot experience peace. Some people go to the temple because they fear that some danger will befall them if they don't worship God. But God is our protector in every way. What we gain from proper worship is complete freedom from fear.

Today, temple worship is only an imitation. The worship isn't done with the understanding of the principles behind it. The son accompanies the father to the temple. The father circumambulates the shrine. The son does the same; he copies everything his father does in the temple. The son grows up and takes his son to the temple. What happened before is repeated. If you ask them why they do all that, they have no answer; and in the temples today no arrangements are made to explain the underlying principles to them.

There was a man who performed puja (ritual worship) every day in the family temple. One day, he got everything ready, and as he began the worship, his cat came in and drank the milk meant for the puja. The next day, as he got ready for the puja, he placed the cat under a basket. Only after the puja was over did he set the cat free[17].

---

[17] God is, of course, present in that cat also. But while we worship God in a particular form, external purity is important, because external purity leads to internal purity.

He made it a practice to put the cat under a basket every day before he started the puja. The years went by in this way. When he died, his son took over the family puja. He continued the ritual of putting a basket over the cat. One day, he got everything ready for the puja and looked for the cat. The cat could not be found. He discovered that the cat had died. He didn't waste any time. He brought a cat from he neighbor's house and put it under a basket, and only then did he proceed with the puja!

The son never asked his father why the cat was placed under the basket. He simply followed his father's practice, without looking for the reason behind it. Today, most people observe rituals in the same way. They never try to learn the principles behind the rituals; they just repeat what others have done before them. Whatever our religion may be, we should try to learn the reasons behind the different rituals. This is what needs to be done now. If we do this, any rituals that are meaningless will not survive. If such rituals are still practiced, we can consciously eliminate them.

There should be a system in the temples to explain spirituality and the principles behind the observances associated with the temples. Temples should become centers that foster a spiritual culture in people. In this way we can reclaim our brilliant heritage.

Question: What is the need of making various offerings in the temple?

Amma: God doesn't need anything from us. What does the Lord of the Universe lack? Why would the sun need a candle?

The true offering to God is to go through life with awareness of the spiritual principles. Eating and sleeping only according to our needs, speaking only when necessary, speaking in a manner that doesn't hurt anyone, not wasting time unnecessarily, caring for the aged and speaking to them lovingly, helping children to get an education, in the absence of a regular job learning a trade to be done at home and spending some of the income to help the poor – all these are different forms of prayer. When we bring proper awareness into our every thought, word, and deed, life itself is transformed into worship. This, indeed, is the true offering to God. But most people are unable to grasp this because they haven't understood the scriptures properly. These days there are few adequate opportunities available to learn about Sanatana Dharma. There are plenty of temples, and many people work there, but arrangements need to be made so that knowledge of the culture can be imparted to the people. People would benefit greatly from this. The effect of this deficiency can be seen in society today.

It is good to shed tears for God while praying, whatever our objectives may be. This will lead us to the highest good. A baby may not be able to say "daddy" properly, but the father will understand what the child means. He knows the baby's mistake is made out of ignorance. God hears us, no matter how we pray. God looks only at our hearts. He cannot turn away from our heartfelt prayers.

When we hear about offerings at the temple, payasam and other things offered to the deity during puja immediately spring to mind. Some people ask, "When poor people are starving, how can we offer sweet dishes to God?" But we don't actually see any deity consuming the payasam. We are the ones who consume it afterwards. The devotees share the payasam that is offered at the temple. Thus the poor and children all get the chance to enjoy the food. It is their satisfaction that comes to us as a blessing. Even though we ourselves like payasam, our hearts expand when we share it with others. We derive joy from that expansiveness of heart. This is the true grace we receive from making offerings at the temple.

Everything we do is done to earn God's grace. So, we should do everything as an offering to Him. The farmer prays before sowing seeds, because there is always a limitation to human effort. For an action to be truly complete and for it to yield fruit, God's grace is needed. The rice is planted; it grows and yields a crop. But if there is a flood just before the harvest, all is lost. Whatever the action, it is made complete through divine grace. This is why our ancestors handed down the tradition of having the attitude of surrendering everything to God first, and implementing or accepting it only then. Even when we eat, the first morsel is offered to God. This is the attitude of surrendering and sharing. In this way we adopt the attitude of considering life not as our own, but as something to be shared with others. It is also a process of surrendering whatever the mind is attached to.

If we ask ourselves what our minds are attached to, most of us know the answer. Ninety percent of our attachments are to wealth. When the family property is divided, we don't hesitate to drag even our mothers to court if our share of the land has ten coconut trees fewer than those of our siblings. Before an Indian man marries a woman, her family history is considered as well as her family's wealth. The exceptions to this are rare, just a few that can be counted on our fingers. So, wealth is what the mind is most attached to, and it's not easy to detach the mind from this. A simple way to do this is to dedicate the mind to God. When we offer our mind to God it is purified. We offer God the things that are dear to us as a way of surrendering the mind.

Some say that Krishna was very fond of payasam. But Krishna is sweetness! – the sweetness of love. We love payasam, and because we offer it to Krishna, we believe he is really fond of it. But it is an offering of something that we ourselves like. In essence, the Lord is love. He delights in the payasam of our hearts, in our love.

The Eternal Truth

A devotee bought a lot of grapes, apples, and different kinds of sweets and placed them in his puja room as an offering to the Lord. "Lord," he said, "see how many things I have brought you: apples, grapes, and sweets! Are you satisfied?"

He heard a voice that said, "No, those are not the things that satisfy me."

"Oh, Lord, tell me what would please you! I will buy it for you."

"There is a flower called the flower of the mind. That is what I want."

"Where will I find it?"

"In the nearest house."

The devotee went straight to the house next door, but the neighbors knew nothing about such a flower. He went to all the houses in the village. Everyone gave the same answer: "We haven't seen or heard of such a flower." Finally the devotee returned to the Lord, prostrated, and said, "Lord, please forgive me! I looked everywhere in the village but I couldn't find the flower you wanted. I have only my heart to offer you!"

"That is the flower I asked for, the flower of your mind. Until now, whatever you have offered me are things that were created by my power. Without the help of my power, you cannot lift even your hand. Everything in the world is my creation. But there is one thing that you have created: the attitude of 'I' (the ego). That is what you should surrender to me. Your innocent mind is the flower I prefer above all else."

When we grasp the divine principles, God's qualities will manifest in us. Amma remembers the old days. Before making a pilgrimage to Sabarimala, the villagers made rice gruel and a special vegetable curry and fed everyone who came. Before they lifted the special pilgrimage bags onto their heads, they gave away handfuls of coins to the children. When we make others happy by giving sumptuous food to the poor or money to children for candy, for example, it comes back to us in the form of satisfaction. The loving-kindness we show to others returns to us as grace.

You may ask why one should offer flowers to God. But that is not just a ritual; there is a practical aspect to it as well. Many people grow flowers for offering to God. It provides those who pick the flowers and those who sell them with a livelihood. It also gives satisfaction to those who buy the flowers and offer them to the Divine. So the flowers that blossom today and wither tomorrow are providing many people with a livelihood, and those who buy them and offer them in worship are given satisfaction. Furthermore, those plants are carefully conserved in nature. We have to look at the utility of everything in this manner. We may ask, Isn't a garland made of cloth better than a flower garland? Those garlands are also good, and keep many people employed. But such garlands do not perish quickly. The real flowers blossom today, wither, and fall away tomorrow. We can make the utmost use of them this way.

The cash offering we make at the temple is not a bribe; it symbolizes our love for God. To give something to someone we love is the face of love. When love is expressed outwardly, it becomes loving-kindness. We love God, but only when we offer something to God is that love transformed into compassion for the world. Only those who do this receive God's grace.

We will usually obey whatever the person we love the most says. A young man is told to quit smoking by the woman he loves. If he sincerely loves her, he will put a stop to his bad habit. That is love. On the other hand, if he argues with her and wants to know why he should obey her, then there is no real love present. In love there are not two individuals. Amma has seen many people give up bad habits in this way. They say, "She doesn't like my drinking! She doesn't like the clothes I wear!" You may ask if it isn't a weakness to adjust to the ones you love. But, in love, this is not a weakness. You cannot enjoy love if reason and logic come into it. In love, there is only love itself; there's no room for logic.

Those who sincerely love God will give up bad habits. They won't do anything that God wouldn't like. Or if they make a mistake, they try their best not to repeat it. They save the money they formerly used to spend on bad habits and use it to help those in need, because serving the poor is the real way of worshipping God. They limit their use of luxuries, and use the money saved in this way to serve the poor. They get into the habit of limiting the use of anything to no more than what is needed. They give up the craving to amass wealth. They give up any thoughts of getting rich by exploiting others. Thus, they maintain the balance and harmony in society.

What we need is not gymnastics in logic but practical common sense. This benefits everyone. There is a saying that telling lies causes blindness.

Our intellect knows that if that were true, there would be only blind people on earth. But when we tell a child that lying causes blindness, he will desist from lying out of fear. Suppose you tell a child who is watching television, "Come here, child. We'll give you immortality!' The child will decline the offer, saying he is happy watching TV. But if he is told, "Run! The house is on fire!" he'll rush out the door in an instant. Those words will make him spring into action. This has nothing to do with the intellect; the words are simply practical. Many practices may appear to be meaningless or superstitious, but when we examine them more subtly, we can see that we get many practical benefits from them. The mind is very limited, indiscriminate, and childish, and these practices guide the mind in the right direction.

A breast-feeding infant cannot digest meat; it would make the baby sick. A baby can only be given simple food. We have to go to each person's level and provide the appropriate guidance. Things should be explained to them in a way that is suitable for their physical, mental, and intellectual constitution. In Sanatana Dharma, there are teachings that are expressed in ways that are suitable for all kinds of people. This is why some things in Sanatana Dharma may appear to be unrefined or even grotesque to some people. But if we examine them logically, we will see how practical they are. It wouldn't be wrong to say that practicality is the foundation of Sanatana Dharma.

Question: We see expensive jewelry being used to adorn the temple images. How can such luxuries be compatible with devotion and spirituality?

Amma: The gold and silver used to decorate the images of God don't belong to a particular individual; they belong to society as a whole. That wealth remains in the temple. Don't most of us buy gold jewelry and keep it at home? Appreciating beauty is part of our nature. We like anything that is beautiful. That is why people wear jewelry and colorful clothes. But this attraction to external things causes bondage; it reinforces the notion that we are the body. If, instead, our attraction to beauty is directed towards God, it will uplift us. When we decorate God's image, we get to enjoy a beauty that is divine. In this way, our minds become focused on God. Even without adornments, God is the quintessence of Beauty. But, normally, we are able to enjoy that beauty only through certain symbols or limiting adjuncts. So, we adorn those images of God according to the way we imagine God.

In olden days, the king was the sovereign of the whole country. But God is the Ruler of the entire universe. People looked upon God in the same way as they viewed the king. They believed that, just as the king provided everything that his subjects required, God provided everything that the universe required. They thought of God as the King of kings. Thus they adorned God's images, the temple images, in a royal manner and found joy in that beauty.

A pot of gold doesn't need any adornments. God doesn't need any decorations. God is the Beauty of all beauty. Even so, decorating a divine image and viewing that beautiful image fills some devotees with joy and a positive atmosphere is created in their hearts. The decorations cultivate devotion within such people.

The effort to see beauty in external objects will remain until one attains the state of jivanmukta[18].[18] People search for beauty everywhere. They wish to be the most beautiful woman or the handsomest man. Since God is perfect Beauty, what could be wrong with wanting to see God (or God's image) in the most beautiful form? God is the all-pervading Consciousness. The devotees know that God is everywhere, within and without. Still, being devotees, they naturally wish to see that captivating form with their own eyes and to enjoy that beauty.

"His lips are sweet, his face is sweet, his eyes are sweet, his smile is sweet, his heart is sweet, his gait is sweet – everything about the Lord of Mathura[19] is sweet[20]!" Thus the devotee sees beauty in everything connected with God, and tries to enjoy that beauty through all the senses: God's form through the eyes, His divine song through the ears, His prasad through the tongue, His fragrance through the nose, and the special unguents (e.g., sandal

---

[18] The state of Self-realization or enlightenment that is attained while still alive.

[19] The Lord of Mathura refers to Krishna. Mathura was the capital of the kingdom that Krishna regained from his wicked uncle Kamsa and restored to the rule of his grandfather.

[20] Madhurashtakam by Sri Sankaracharya

paste) through touch. Thus, each of the senses can be used to focus the mind fully on God.

God is perfectly complete, whether He appears in the form of a king or a beggar. We decorate God according to our imagination, that's all. God cannot be limited to our very limited concepts. Nor is God wanting in anything. It makes no difference to God whatsoever if we decorate His image or not. None of the expensive things offered by the devotees affect God in any way. They are just adornments, mere decorations to satisfy the devotee.

Amma recalls the story of Sri Rama in this context. The decision had been made to proclaim Rama as the crown prince. The preparations for the ceremony were already underway. But suddenly he was asked to go into exile in the forest, and he set out without any change of emotion. Had he wanted to, he could have reigned as king – the people were all on his side – but, even so, he left and never regretted his decision because he wasn't attached to anything. It is this detachment we should gain by worshipping God.

The robber who is taken into custody will be surrounded by police. The prime minister is also surrounded by police. But in the prime minister's case, the police are under his control. If he doesn't want them to be there, he can send them away. The robber, on the other hand, is afraid of the police and is under their control. God is like the prime minister. Everything is under His control. This doesn't change, regardless of what form God assumes. When God manifests on earth as different incarnations, those incarnations behave like humans because they want to be living examples for the world. But this doesn't bind them in any way. They are like butter in water. They are like a ripe peanut in the shell. They are not attached to anything, nor can anything stick to them.

Question: There is the practice of offering substances like honey and clarified butter to the fire during a homa (sacred fire ritual) in order to attain God's grace. Is it right to waste things in this way? It is said that many expensive materials are offered into the fire. What is Amma's view on this?

Amma: Amma doesn't approve of offering expensive materials into the fire. If that has been done, it may have been to remove the mind's attachment to those materials. Even so, it is better to give such things away as gifts than to throw them in the fire. That would benefit the poor, and this seems more logical to Amma.

However, there are subtle meanings involved in a homa. It is the ego that is being offered to God. The ego is the creation of the mind, and the homa symbolizes the surrender of the mind to God. We offer into the fire materials that symbolize our senses, because our senses constitute the bondage or attachments of the mind. To receive God's grace, it isn't necessary to perform a ritual in which we offer various objects to the fire. Performing good deeds is all that is needed. It is enough to love and to serve others. God's grace will come to those who have this attitude.

In another sense, the materials offered into the homa fire are not really being wasted. Ceremonies like the homa have been laid down in the part of the Vedas that deals with rituals. Some of the benefits of those rituals have been scientifically proven. The homa benefits nature. When clarified butter, coconut, honey, sesame seeds, karuka grass, and other ingredients are offered into the fire, the smoke from the fire has the power to purify the atmosphere. It disinfects without the use of poisonous chemicals. Those who breathe in the fragrant smoke of the homa benefit as well.

Our ancestors in antiquity started a fire by rubbing special pieces of wood together. This didn't pollute the air the way burning matches do. By lighting the fire at dawn, sitting beside it in a comfortable posture, and performing the homa, we gain concentration of mind. Our thoughts diminish. Mental tension decreases. Sitting next to the fire, the body perspires and the impurities in the body are eliminated. We inhale the fragrance from the burning clarified butter and coconut, and this is good for our health. Simultaneously, the atmosphere is being purified. Every observance and ritual prescribed by our ancestors was meant not only for inner purification but to maintain the harmony of nature. None of the prescribed actions caused any pollution.

In the old days, it was the custom in most homes to light an oil lamp at dusk. Burning a wick placed in oil in a bronze lamp helps purify the atmosphere.

The Eternal Truth

As a child, Amma observed how the smoke from such lamps was collected inside a bowl. The women would mix the soot from this with lime juice, and when a child was born the mixture was applied to the baby's eyes. This destroys the organisms beneath the eyelids without any harmful side effects. That smoke is very different from the smoke from a kerosene lamp.

Most of the customs observed in the old days benefited nature. In the past, when children were vaccinated, their mothers applied cow dung to the injection spot to make it heal quickly. If we were to apply cow dung today, the wound would turn septic. This is how impure cow dung has become. The remedy of the past has become today's poison. In those days, toxic chemicals were not used in agriculture; only leaves and cow dung were used as fertilizer. But, today, most farmers use toxic fertilizers and insecticides. The hay from such farms is fed to the cows, and the dung from those cows is therefore toxic. It would be dangerous to touch a wound with that dung. This is how polluted nature has become.

Amma does not ignore the fact that there may be economic gain to be had from the use of chemical fertilizers. With those chemicals we temporarily get better harvests. But in another way they are killing us. We may argue that the larger crops are a solution to starvation, but we forget the important fact that because people consume vegetables and grains grown using those toxic fertilizers, countless cells in their bodies perish.

We don't take the prick of a small needle very seriously, but if we are continuously pricked it could end in death. The consequence of toxic substances entering our bodies is similar to that. Each of our cells is in the process of dying. Only when we fall dead will we understand the seriousness of the matter. Through our food, water, and air we consume numerous poisons. They make us ill and lead us more rapidly towards death.

We don't realize that many things that are done today in the name of hygiene have negative effects. People use chemical cleaners to clean and disinfect their homes. But, even to breathe in the smell of many of those cleaners is harmful to our health. They also kill beneficial microorganisms. On the other hand, when we perform a homa, the materials offered into the fire kill germs and purify the air. None of these materials have any harmful effects.

Nowadays, we use poisonous chemicals to kill ants. Those pesticides harm not only the ants but also our own cells. But when we breathe in the fragrant air arising from the homa fire, the cells in our bodies become refreshed and healthier. It benefits not only humans, but other living beings and nature as well.

In the past, people used castor oil as a laxative. It wasn't harmful at all. Today, many people use various pills as laxatives. Those substances do act as laxatives, but at the same time they destroy many beneficial bacteria in the body, and there can be other side effects as well. Despite the fact that they know this, many people find it convenient to depend on those laxatives. People tend to consider only what feels most convenient at the moment, and choose to ignore the future consequences.

In the old days, people carried out each action in light of an overall perspective regarding nature. The homa began from this perspective. Amma doesn't mean that everyone should start performing homas. It is enough to use that money for charitable activities. In addition to this, plant ten new trees! This will benefit the atmosphere and help to preserve nature.

Question: Is there any benefit to be gained from singing devotional songs, praying, chanting mantras, etc.? Shouldn't we use that time to do something useful for the world instead?

Amma: Many people sing sensual songs. If we were to say to them, "What's the use of that? Shouldn't you be doing something useful for the world instead?" what would they say to that? Isn't it true that only those who experience the benefit of something can understand it? People enjoy listening to ordinary songs. When the devotee hears God's name being sung, he or she forgets all else and becomes absorbed in the Divine. Ordinary songs are enjoyable because they deal with the emotions of the mind and with worldly relationships. Listeners get absorbed in those sentiments and enjoy it. But when devotional songs and prayers are sung, both the singers and the listeners experience mental peace.

Music such as disco music awakens various emotional waves. Listening to sensual songs awakens the lover-beloved mood and leads to related thoughts and sentiments. Devotional songs, on the other hand, remind us of our relationship with God; divine qualities are awakened instead of worldly emotions. The emotions are quieted and this gives peace to both the singers and the listeners.

Amma doesn't dismiss ordinary songs. Many people enjoy them. There are different kinds of people in the world. Everything has a certain relevance at the level of each individual. So, Amma doesn't reject anything.

When we sing the glories of God, we are not aiming only at the state of God-realization. There are other benefits as well. Devotional songs and prayers engender positive vibrations within us and throughout our surroundings. There is no room in that for any anger or negativity; there is only the sentiment that makes everyone a friend. Through prayer, a process of contemplation takes place in the mind of the devotee. A child repeats a word ten times, commits it to memory, and plants it firmly in the heart. Similarly, when we sing devotional songs, when we sing about God's glories again and again, they become rooted in our hearts and our lives are enriched.

Singing devotional songs makes the mind joyful. It is restful for the mind. To experience this fully we have to develop the attitude "I am nothing. You (God) are everything!" That is true prayer. It is not easy to develop this attitude. The sun has to rise for darkness to disappear. Only with the dawn of knowledge can this mental state blossom fully. We don't have to wait until then; we just need to cultivate the right mental disposition and go forward.

We shouldn't forget that God is our strength. Not even our next breath is under our control. We start walking down the stairs, saying, "I'll be right down" – and yet we hear of people succumbing to a heart attack before they have finished the sentence. So, we need to develop the attitude that we are just instruments in God's hands.

We shouldn't pray or sing devotional songs just to have our desires fulfilled. There are many who think of prayer as a means for personal gain. The aim of prayer is to awaken positive qualities and good vibrations within. If life is lived just to satisfy one's desires, robberies, murders, and rapes will increase. Because there are police, and people fear the police, there is at least some limit on crime in society. But it is love that helps people to truly stay on the right path – love and devotion for God. This is the practical way to maintain harmony in society. Prayer accompanied by positive thoughts produces good vibrations. Prayer accompanied by negative thoughts produces bad vibrations. The vibrations around a person who is praying will depend on the nature of his or her prayer. If the person prays about harming an adversary, the person praying will be filled with vibrations of anger – and what the world gets from that person is anger. Thus, the vibrations that emanate to the world from a praying individual match the attitude behind his or her prayer.

Different emotions arise in a person when he thinks of his mother, his wife, and his children. When he remembers his mother, maternal love and affection fill his mind. Thoughts about his wife may bring forth conjugal sentiments and feelings about the sharing of hearts. Thinking about his children, he feels parental love. All these feelings reside in the mind, and they awaken different vibrations. Because the vibrations depend on one's state of mind, we should make sure that our prayers are always accompanied by positive thoughts. Only then will our prayers be of any benefit to us and to society as a whole. Prayer accompanied by good thoughts, without any feelings of anger or vengeance, not only removes mental tension but also creates a positive atmosphere both within and without.

Thoughts are like a contagious virus. If you go near a person suffering from a fever, you, too, may catch a fever because the germs carrying the illness may be passed on to you. If you go to a place where perfume bottles are filled, your body will pick up the fragrance. Similarly, there are subtle vibrations created wherever God's glory is sung. Those vibrations will spread to our aura. But our hearts have to open for this to happen. Only then can we enjoy this and be energized. If the mind has a negative attitude, we won't be benefited.

Even in a spiritual environment, people's interests are often limited to the plane of the senses. That is why some people don't receive the grace of the spiritual masters whom they approach and who may even mentally bestow blessings upon them. A frog that lives under a lotus isn't aware of the flower, nor can it enjoy its fragrance. Even around the udder filled with milk, the mosquitoes are attracted only to blood.

Some people cannot see the changes taking place in those who practice spiritual teachings. They see only the defects in everything. There are those who criticize Hinduism by pointing to the animal sacrifices that were once practiced in the name of religion. Listening to them, it would seem that Hinduism consists only of animal sacrifice! In the past, when asked to sacrifice the animal within themselves (the ego), there were some people who, out of ignorance, offered actual live animals as a sacrifice. But, today, don't we see modern people, clai-ming to know the Truth, conducting human sacrifices all over the world? Think of how many are being killed in the name of religion and politics! We claim to have risen above our ancestors, when, in fact, we have not. The upward progress we show is actually leading to our downfall. To understand this, we need to see the situation from its entire perspective; we have to see it from a bird's eye view, for if we look from below, we will see only a very limited side.

Most people belong to a political party. They may be attracted to the party because of the lives of the leaders and their idealism and sacrifices. Having adopted those ideals, they may have started working for the party. However, it would be even better if they were to adopt spiritual ideals, for in those principles there is no anger or vengeance, and no selfishness. Where can we find loftier ideals than those of the Bhagavad Gita?

There are those who may ask, "Doesn't Krishna say in the Gita that we have to surrender everything and work without remuneration?" But hardly anyone thinks about why the Lord said that. If seeds are sown, they may or may not sprout. If there is no rain, you can dig wells and get water for irrigation; but however much you try, you cannot say for sure how good the harvest will be. Just before the harvest, a great storm or a flood could destroy the entire crop. This is the nature of the world. If we can accept this, we can live without sorrow. This is why Krishna said, "Perform your work. The result is in God's hands. Do not worry about it!" However great our effort may be, God's grace is also needed if we are to get the proper fruits of our actions. This is what He taught, not that we shouldn't demand or receive any wages for our work.

If you sincerely believe that instead of singing the glories of God, praying, or chanting His names, it is enough to do actions that benefit the world, then that is actually enough. God isn't someone sitting beyond the sky. God is everywhere. The Creator and creation are not two different things. The gold and the gold chain are not different – there is gold in the chain and the chain is gold. God is within us, and we are in God. Indeed, the greatest thing is to see God in all human beings and to worship them. But the mind has to embrace this attitude one hundred percent. It is very difficult to perform actions in a perfectly selfless way. Selfishness will creep in without our knowledge, and then we won't receive the full benefit of that selfless action.

People may say, "Let's not talk about bosses and workers. Let's have equality!" But how many bosses are willing to include their workers in their own class? Is the leader who talks about workers' rights willing to give up his chair to a follower? Selflessness has to do with actions, not with words. But this doesn't happen in one day, for it needs constant practice. We need to remember to fill each breath with good thoughts. We should try to cultivate good qualities. When we do this, our breath will create good vibrations in the atmosphere. It is often said that factories pollute the air, but there is an even greater poison within the human being, and that is the ego. That should be feared above all else. Devotional singing and prayers help purify the minds that carry such poisons.

It is hard to stop a cow that is running away by running after it. If you instead hold some fodder that the cow likes in your outstretched hand and call it, the cow will come to you, and then you can easily tether the animal. Likewise, chanting a mantra will help us bring the mind under control.

Even though we are one with the Creator, at present our minds are not under our control and so we are not aware of that oneness. We need to take control of the mind in the same way as we use the remote control of a television set to select a desired channel. Today our minds are running after many different things. Chanting the divine names is an easy way to bring back the wayward mind and to make it focus on God.

Through spiritual practice, the mind develops the ability to adjust to any situation. People tend to be tense. Repeating a mantra is an exercise that removes our tension. In the old days, children used certain seeds to learn how to count. Using the seeds, they practiced "one, two, three," etc. Later they could count in their minds without the aid of the seeds. When a forgetful person goes shopping, he or she will bring a list; when the items are purchased, the list can be thrown away. In a similar way, we are presently in a state of forgetfulness; we are not awakened. Until awakening takes place, repeating a mantra and other spiritual practices are necessary.

Just as there are rules for everything, there are certain rules for meditation and other spiritual practices. Anyone can sing ordinary songs, but without musical training, you cannot give a classical music concert. There are rules for concert playing. Similarly, one needs some training to meditate successfully. Meditation is very practical, but problems can arise if one isn't careful to do it in a productive way.

A health tonic is good for the body. But, if instead of the prescribed dose of a teaspoon, you drink the whole bottle, it could harm you; or if you swallow two spoonfuls instead of the prescribed five, that won't help either. You need to stick to the prescribed dose. Similarly, you should meditate according to your spiritual master's directions. There are some spiritual practices are not suitable for everyone. If such practices are done by the wrong person, he or she may be unable to sleep, may even become violent, and develop certain physical disorders. So, it can be dangerous if one isn't careful. However, there are no such problems with singing devotional songs, chanting, or praying. Anyone can do these practices safely. With meditation more care is needed. With meditation, the seeker needs the master's help. A space craft can lift off from the earth, overcoming the earth's gravity, but it often needs a second rocket, a booster rocket, to fire in order to adjust its course and continue its journey. Similarly, a boost from the master's guidance is essential for progress on the spiritual journey.

Each of us has the power to be God or a demon. We can be Krishna or Jarasandha[21].21 Both qualities are within us: love and anger. Our nature will be determined by which of those qualities we choose to nurture. So we need to cultivate good thoughts, free from any spirit of anger, and a clear mind, free from conflict. Through prayer and the repetition of a mantra, we can remove the negativities from our minds and completely forget the unessential

---

[21] Jarasandha was a powerful but unrighteous king who ruled the land of Magadha in Krishna's time. He subjugated more than one hundred kingdoms. He was defeated repeatedly in several wars he waged against Krishna. Later, Bhima, following Krishna's counsel, killed Jarasandha in a fight between the two of them.

things. Normally, we forget things when we are unconscious, and when we regain our awareness we remember them again; this brings back our tension. But what happens through spiritual practices is different, for in spiritual practice we forget what isn't wanted while we are fully awake.

By pasting a three-word poster on a wall saying "Stick no bills," we can avoid hundreds of words. It is true that our notice itself is a poster, but it serves a larger purpose. Chanting a mantra is similar. By chanting a mantra, we reduce the number of thoughts. When other thoughts are kept away, the tension that normally arises from those thoughts is removed. At least while chanting, the mind is calm; there is no anger or negativity. The mind is purified. Selfishness decreases and we gain expansiveness of mind. We also create good vibrations in nature.

If the water that flows through many different channels is directed into one channel, we can use it to produce electric power. Through mantra repetition and meditation, we can control the power of the mind, which is otherwise lost in a multitude of thoughts. In this way, we can conserve and build up our energy.

A porter gets a higher education and becomes a scientist. The scientist still uses the same head that previously carried loads of luggage. But is the ability of the porter the same as that of the scientist? If a porter can become a scientist, why shouldn't an ordinary person be able to blossom into a spiritual being? This is possible through spiritual practice, an attitude of selflessness, and good thoughts. One can accumulate a great deal of spiritual power by concentrating the mind. The power gained through mantra chanting can be used in a way that will benefit the world. There is no selfishness in that. The world receives only good words and deeds from such individuals.

All spiritual practices are done to develop in us the attitude of wanting to dedicate ourselves to the world. But Amma is ready to worship the feet of those who don't have the inclination to practice any spiritual discipline but are nevertheless willing to dedicate their lives to the world. The benefit gained through prayer can also be gained through selfless service. In selflessness one is complete. In that state, the limited individual disappears.

The Eternal Truth

Question: Some people cry when they pray. Isn't this a sign of weakness? Don't we just lose our energy when we cry like that?

Amma: Shedding tears while praying is not a weakness. When we cry for ordinary things it is like a piece of firewood uselessly burning up; but when we weep in prayer, it is like using that burning firewood to make payasam – it gives us sweetness. As a candle burns down, its brightness increases. When we shed tears about material things, it may perhaps help lighten the load in our hearts, but we shouldn't waste our time crying about what is gone or what is yet to come. "Will my child study hard enough and pass the examination?" "Look what those people did to me!" "What will the neighbors say?" To sit and cry about such things can be considered a weakness. It will only lead to depression and other mental disorders. However, when we open our hearts and pray to God, it gives us peace and mental quietude.

When we pray out of our longing for God, positive qualities are nurtured within us. Heartfelt prayer in which we cry for God steadies and focuses the mind, and the mind becomes one-pointed. Instead of losing energy, we gain energy through such concentration. Even though God is within us, our minds are not focused on God. Crying in prayer is a way of focusing the mind on God.

When a toddler says he is hungry, the mother may not respond immediately. But what happens when the child starts crying? The mother will come running, ready to pick up and feed her child. Similarly, to shed tears while praying is a good way to gain control over the mind. It is certainly not a weakness.

A seeker on the path of self-inquiry asserts, "I am not the mind, intellect, or body; I am not merit or demerit – I am the pure Self." This process of negation is done with the mind. For those who haven't learned meditation, yoga, or the scriptures, an easy way to control the mind is to tell everything to God with an open heart, to cry and pray for the realization of the Truth. This is also a form of negation because, instead of saying "I am not this, I am not that," we are saying to God, "You are everything."

The Eternal Truth

Some people like to read silently. Others have to read aloud in order to understand the words. There are those who enjoy singing aloud, while others enjoy humming softly. Each person chooses what suits him or her. It would be wrong to label any of those choices as weaknesses. It is a matter of personal choice, that's all.

God is within you, but your mind isn't attuned to this. Say that there is a pot in front of you. Even if your eyes are open, if your mind is elsewhere, you won't see the pot. You can't hear someone speaking if your mind isn't present. In the same way, even though God is within us, we do not know Him because our minds are not focused within – we are not looking inward. Normally, the mind is tied to a lot of things. We have to bring the mind back and focus it on God. In this way we can cultivate God's qualities within us, qualities such as love, compassion, and equal vision. We should develop those qualities within ourselves and around us, so that others will be benefited. Prayer has the same effect.

One of Amma's children said to Amma, "I don't like to pray. What's the use of praying?" Amma said, "Let Amma ask you something. Say that you are in love. Will you dislike talking to your beloved?

Won't you enjoy it? To the devotee, this is what praying is like. To the devotee, God is everything. And if someone were to disapprove of your talking to your beloved, how would you react? Would you care what that person thinks? Your statement about prayer is like that person's criticism. The love we feel for God is no ordinary love. It is something so utterly sacred."

Love and devotion for God cannot be compared to any ordinary love relationship. A man craves a woman's love, and a woman craves love from a man. In that love, they enjoy each other. But they don't experience fullness or perfection, because they are both beggars. The devotee's prayer to God is different. The devotee prays for the grace to develop God's qualities within and the broad-mindedness to see and love everyone as God. The devotee shares the feelings of her heart with God for this purpose. She not only nurtures godly qualities within, but also transforms her life into something that benefits others. Ordinary people share their feelings with many others; they crave to be loved by others. But the devotee shares her heart only with the indwelling God, praying, "Let me be like You!

Give me the strength to love all beings, and the strength to forgive!"

Devotional singing is the absolute delight of the devotee's heart; it is the devotee's form of indulgence. Worldly people find their pleasure in external things, but internal delight is different, and it is harmless. Once you have experienced it, you will no longer go in search of external indulgence. If you get delicious food at home, will you go looking for it elsewhere? In prayer, we look within for a place of rest. This is not like a candle that has to be lit with external help; it is a light that shines spontaneously. It is a path on which we discover the light shining within ourselves.

In the material world, people seek satisfaction through desire. But it is prayer that leads to peace of mind. You may experience some peace from the material world, but it is never permanent. If your loved ones ignore you, you feel sad. If one person doesn't want to talk, the other one feels sad. People go sear-ching for happiness, and when they don't succeed in finding it, more sorrow follows. When we share our sorrows with others, they respond by talking about their own sorrows. We go to someone in search of solace,

The Eternal Truth

but come back loaded with twice as much sorrow! Like the spider that builds its web and then dies in it, people with these attachments end up bound by them. It is like a small snake trying to swallow a big frog! To be released from this condition you have to develop the attitude of a witness. This is also the aim of prayer.

There were two women who were neighbors. The husband of one of them died. In her grief, the widow wailed loudly. The other woman came over to console her, saying, "Who is free from death? If not today, it will happen tomorrow. The electric current doesn't get destroyed even if the bulb fails. In the same way, the Self cannot be destroyed even if the body perishes." With words of this kind, she consoled the weeping woman. After some time, the second woman's son died. She wept uncontrollably. The widow came over and said to her grieving friend, "Aren't you the one who came and consoled me when my husband died? Do you remember what you said to me then?" But no matter what the widow said, she couldn't stop her bereaved friend from crying. The woman who lost her son was completely identified with her own grief. Yet, when her neighbor had lost her husband, she had been able to stand apart and look at her friend's situation as a witness – and she had been able to console her to a certain extent; she had given her strength.

Whenever we identify with a situation, our suffering increases. But when we view a situation from the witness point of view, our inner strength grows. We read about a plane crash in the paper. If our children or relatives were on that flight, we won't be able to read the next line because of our grief. If there is no possibility that our loved ones were on that plane, our eyes will casually finish reading the story and then wander over to the next piece of news.

In worldly relationships we may experience suffering. If one person's love diminishes, the other person may get angry. The reason is that the relationship is based on wishes and hopes, on desires and expectations. But when we cry for God, it is completely different because we don't expect anything in return for our love. And, yet, in that love without expectations we are given everything. In real prayer we say, "God, give us your qualities and the strength to do selfless service!"

Schoolchildren are often asked to write down a fact or a passage again and again so that they will remember it. If they write a forgotten lesson ten times, they won't forget it again; it becomes firmly fixed in their memory. Similarly, when we contemplate the divine qualities repeatedly during our prayers, we are making those qualities our own; we are fixing them in our consciousness. The devotee who awakens these qualities within him- or herself is not bound by them but rises to a state beyond all qualities. The one who is beyond all qualities is not bound to anything. Such a person remains a witness. By nurturing the divine qualities within, we forget ourselves and are able to love and help others. Then the limited individual is no longer there. This is a state beyond all qualities.

Question: Some people describe the Shiva linga[22] as obscene. Is there any basis for this?

---

[22] An elongated oval stone; the principle of creativity; often worshipped as a symbol of Lord Shiva.

Amma: My children, people talk that way only because they do not understand the principle behind the Shiva linga. Each individual sees either good or bad in everything depending on that person's own inner tendencies.

Each religion and organization has its own symbols or emblems. The fabric used to make the flag of a country or a political party may cost no more than ten rupees – but think of the value that is given to the flag! In that flag, people see their country or their party. For the party workers, the flag symbolizes the ideals of their party. If someone were to spit on that cloth or tear it to pieces saying it's worth no more than ten rupees, there would be a serious conflict. When you see a flag, you don't think about the cotton it is made of. You don't think about the excreta that has been used as fertilizer to grow that cotton, and how foul-smelling it must have been. In that flag you only see the ideals of the country or the political party it represents.

For Amma's Christian children, the cross is a symbol of sacrifice. When we pray in front of the cross, we don't think of the fact that it was the instrument used to crucify criminals. We see it as the symbol of Christ's sacrifice and compassion.

When Amma's Muslim children prostrate towards Mecca, they are thinking of divine qualities.

We cannot understand why some people ridicule and insult the divine symbols and images of the Hindu faith. The Shiva linga isn't a symbol of one particular religion; it actually stands for a scientific principle.

Many symbols are used in mathematics and science; for example, as the signs for multiplication and division. Don't people of all religions and countries use those symbols? No one asks what religion the inventor of those symbols belonged to. No one discards the symbols on such grounds. Everyone who wants to learn mathematics accepts those symbols. Similarly, no one who really understands the principle behind the Shiva linga can reject it.

My children, the meaning of the word linga is 'the place of dissolution.' The universe arises out of the linga and finally dissolves into it. The Rishis of anti-quity looked for the origin of the universe and, through the austerities they performed, they discovered that Brahman, the Absolute Reality, is the Source and Support of everything. Brahman cannot be described in words. One cannot point to Brahman. The beginning and end of everything lies in That. Brahman, the abode of all attributes and qualities, is devoid of attributes and qualities, and devoid of form. How can the attributeless be described? Only that which has attributes can be grasped by the mind and the senses. In this difficult context, the sages found a symbol to represent that initial stage between Brahman and Creation: the Shiva linga. It signifies the creation of the universe out of Brahman. The Shiva linga is the symbol the Rishis used to reveal the Truth they experienced in a way that ordinary people could understand. We need to understand that the attributeless Ultimate Reality is beyond name, form, and individuality, but that people need to meditate on and worship that Ultimate Reality in an accessible way. The Rishis accepted the Shiva linga as a scientific symbol to be used in this way.

Scientists who study certain rays that cannot be seen by the eye use symbols to describe them to others. When we hear about X-rays, we know they are a certain type of radiation. Similarly, when we see the Shiva linga, we understand it is the attributeless Brahman represented in its aspect with attributes.

The word shiva means 'auspicious.' Auspiciousness doesn't have a form. By worshipping the Shiva linga, which is a symbol of auspiciousness, the worshipper receives that which is auspicious. Auspiciousness doesn't make any distinctions such as caste. Whoever worships the linga, with the awareness of the principle behind it, will benefit.

My children, at the beginning of creation, the Ultimate Principle separated into prakriti and purusha[23]. By the word prakriti, the Rishis meant the universe that we can know and experience. Even though purusha normally means 'male,' that's not what it signifies here. Purusha is Self-awareness. Prakriti and purusha are not two; they are one. Like fire and its power to burn, they cannot be separated. When the word purusha is mentioned, those who haven't studied spirituality think of 'male.' This is why the Supreme Self, which is pure Consciousness, was assigned the male form and given the name Shiva. And prakriti was thought of as female and given the names Shakti and Devi.

Every movement has an underlying motionless substratum, just as a pestle functions on the unmoving base of a mortar. Shiva is the motionless principle underlying every movement in the universe,

---

[23] The consciousness that dwells within the body; the pure, unblemished Universal Consciousness/Existence.

while Shakti is the Power that is the cause of all movement. The Shiva linga is the symbol of the unity of Shiva and Shakti. When we meditate on this symbol with concentration, that Ultimate Truth will be awakened within us.

We should also consider why the Shiva linga was given its form. Today scientists say that the universe is egg-shaped. In India, for thousands of years, the universe was referred to as Brahmandam, meaning 'the great egg.' Brahman means the absolute greatest. The Shiva linga is a microcosm of that vast cosmic egg. When we worship the Shiva linga, we are, in fact, worshipping the entire universe as the Auspicious Form and as the Divine Consciousness. This is not the worship of a God who sits somewhere beyond the sky. This teaches us that any selfless service rendered to the universe, including to all living beings, is worship of Shiva.

Today, our condition is that of a baby bird sitting inside the eggshell of the ego. The fledgling can only dream of the freedom of the skies but cannot experience it. To experience that freedom, the egg has to hatch in the warmth beneath the mother bird's body, so that the fledgling can emerge. Similarly, for us to enjoy the bliss of the Self, the shell of the ego has to break. The egg-shaped Shiva linga awakens the awareness of this truth in the worshipper.

We sing, "Akasha linga pahi mam, atma linga pahi mam," etc. The words' literal meaning is "Sky linga, protect me; Self linga protect me." The real meaning of this is, "May God, who is all-pervading like the sky, protect me; may the Supreme Self, which is my own real nature, protect me!"

So, the meaning of linga is not 'phallus,' for not even fools would pray to a male's sexual organs for protection!

My children, who benefits from ascribing a non-existent meaning to and ridiculing a divine symbol that countless millions of people throughout the ages have used for the upliftment of their souls? This causes only anger and conflict.

The Puranas[24] say that Lord Shiva burned Kama, the god of lust, in the fire of his third eye. Today, we consider material things to be real, everlasting, and belonging to us. We focus only on such things. Only when the third eye of knowledge is opened do we realize that all of that is perishable, and that

---

[24] Divine epics, depicting the lives of the gods.

only the Self is everlasting. Then we can enjoy supreme bliss. In that state, there is no difference between male and female, mine and yours. This is what is meant by saying that Kama was destroyed. The Shiva linga helps us to grasp this principle and frees the mind from lust. This is why the Shiva linga was worshipped by both men and women, the old and the young, the Brahmin and the outcast.

Only a mind deluded by lust can possibly see the Shiva linga as a symbol of lust. We should explain the true principle behind the symbol to such people and thus uplift their minds.

The Shiva linga illustrates that Shiva and Shakti are not two, but one and the same. This is relevant in family life as well. The husband and wife should be of one mind. If the man is the support of the family, the woman is the Shakti, the strength of the family. There is probably no other symbol of the equality and love between a man and a woman. This is why the Shiva linga is given so much importance in the Brahmasthanam temples that Amma has established.

The Eternal Truth

Question: It is said that Shiva dwells in funeral grounds. What is the meaning of this?

Amma: Desire is the cause of human suffering. The reason the mind runs after each desire is the perception, "I am not complete." You will never experience perfect peace if you focus only on acquiring material gains. At the cremation grounds, all material desires and the body, which is the instrument used to fulfill those desires, are reduced to ashes. And there, where those desires are absent and there is no body-consciousness, Lord Shiva dances in bliss. That is why he is called the resident of the cremation grounds. The meaning of this is not that bliss comes to us only after death. Everything is within us. We and the universe are one; both are equally complete. But when the attachment to the body dies in the fire of Self-awareness, we are automatically filled with bliss.

Shiva's body is decorated with ashes from the funeral pyres. This is the symbol of having conquered all desires. Also, when you put holy ash[25] on your forehead, it is of great medical benefit. Furthermore, the mind becomes aware of the perishable nature of the body. This inspires us to remember that this body will soon perish, and that we should do good deeds as soon as possible, before the body dies.

Shiva is called 'the detached one' (vairagi). Detachment (vairagya) means absence of attachment. Children place a lot of importance on their toys, while for adults those same toys don't mean anything. Detachment means not giving undue importance to name or position, bodily comforts, family or friends. If we don't develop true detachment, our happiness will depend on the tips of other peoples' tongues! Our life becomes a puppet in the hands of others. Dispassion is what gives us true freedom. If we have dispassion, nothing in the world can conceal the bliss that is innate in us. Shiva, who wears ashes and resides in the funeral grounds, teaches us this principle. This is why Lord Shiva is considered the first among Gurus.

---

[25] Holy ash (bhasmam, vibhuti) is traditionally made of dried cow dung that is burned to ashes.

Glossary

Advaita – Non-dualism. The philosophy which teaches that the Creator and creation are one and indivisible.

Archana – 'Offering for worship.' A form of worship in which the names of a deity are chanted, usually 108, 300, or 1000 names in one sitting.

Ashram – 'Place of striving.' A place where spiritual aspirants live or visit in order to lead a spiritual life and engage in spiritual practice. It is usually the home of a spiritual master, saint, or ascetic, who guides the aspirants.

Asura – A demon; a person with demonic qualities.

Atman – The transcendental Self, Spirit, or Consciousness, which is eternal; our essential nature. One of the fundamental tenets of Sanatana Dharma is that we are the eternal, pure, unblemishable Self (Spirit).

Avadhut(a) – A Self-realized soul who doesn't follow social conventions. By conventional standards, avadhuts are considered extremely eccentric.

Bhagavad Gita – 'Song of the Lord.' Bhagavad = of the Lord; gita = song; referring particularly to advice. The teachings that Krishna gave Arjuna on the Kurukshetra battlefield at the beginning of the Mahabharata war. It is a practical guide for the daily life of everyone, and contains the essence of Vedic wisdom. Commonly referred to as the Gita.

Bhagavan – The Lord; God. One endowed with six divine qualities or bhagas: eight siddhis (powers), strength, glory, good fortune, supreme knowledge, and dispassion.

Bhagavatam – One of eighteen scriptures known as the Puranas, dealing especially with the incarnations of Vishnu, and, in great detail, with the life of Sri Krishna. It emphasizes the path of devotion. Also known as the Srimad Bhagavatam.

Bhajan – Devotional song; devotional singing.

Bhakti – Devotion.

Bhakti Yoga – 'Union through devotion.' The path of love and devotion. The way of attaining Self-realization through devotion and complete surrender to God.

Bhava – Divine mood, attitude, or state.

Brahma, Vishnu, and Maheswara (Shiva) – The three aspects of God, associated with creation, preservation, and dissolution.

Brahman – The Absolute Reality; the Whole; Supreme Being; 'That' which encompasses and pervades everything, which is One and indivisible.

Brahmandam – 'The great egg'; the universe.

Brahmasthanam Temple – 'The Abode of Brahman.' Born out of Amma's divine intuition, these unique temples are the first to show multiple deities on a single stone. The stone is four-sided, displaying Ganesha, Shiva, Devi and Rahu, emphasizing the inherent unity underlying the manifold aspects of the Divine. There are sixteen such temples throughout India and one in Mauritius.

Brahma Sutras – Aphorisms by Sage Badarayana (Veda Vyasa) expounding Vedantic philosophy.

Brahmin – In the Indian caste system the Brahmins were the priests and teachers.

Darshan – An audience with or a vision of the Divine or a holy person.

Deva – 'The shining one.' A god or celestial being that exists on the astral plane, in a subtle, non-physical body.

Devi – 'The Effulgent One.' The Goddess, the Divine Mother.

Dharma – From the root dhri; to support, uphold, hold onto. Often translated simply as 'righteousness.' Dharma has many profoundly interrelated meanings: that which upholds the universe, the laws of Truth, the universal laws, the laws of nature, in accordance with divine harmony, righteousness, religion, duty, responsibility, right conduct, justice, goodness, and truth. Dharma signifies the inner principles of religion. It signifies the true nature, proper functions and actions of a being or object. It is, for example, the dharma of fire to burn. The dharma of a human being is to live in harmony with the universal spiritual principles and to cultivate a higher consciousness.

Durga – A name of the Goddess, the Divine Mother. She is often depicted as wielding a number of weapons and riding a lion. She is the destroyer of evil and the protector of the good. She destroys the desires and negative tendencies (vasanas) of her children, and unveils to them the Supreme Spirit.

Ganesha – The son of Shiva and Parvati. Ganesha removes obstacles and bestows success. He is worshipped at the beginning of all ceremonies and before the beginning of any new undertaking. Ganesha is elephant-headed and his vehicle is a mouse. This represents the fact that God exists in all creatures, from the largest to the smallest; it also symbolizes the conquering of all desires. The visual details of Ganesha indicate deep philosophical meanings, which are meant to guide the spiritual aspirant.

Gita – Song. See Bhagavad Gita.

Guru – 'One who removes the darkness of ignorance.' Spiritual master/guide.

Gurukula – An ashram with a living guru, where disciples live and study with the guru. In the olden days, the gurukulas were boarding schools where youngsters were given a comprehensive education based on the Vedas.

Hatha Yoga – A system of physical and mental exercises developed in ancient times, with the purpose of making the body and its vital functions into perfect instruments in order to help one attain Self-realization.

Homa – Sacred fire ritual.

Ishwara – God. The personal aspect of the Absolute Reality; the One who controls; the causal point of creation.

Japa – Repetition of a mantra, a prayer, or one of God's names.

Jivanmukta – The state of Self-realization or enlightenment that is attained while one is still alive.

Jnana – 'Knowledge.' Supreme knowledge is a direct experience, beyond any possible perception of the limited mind, intellect, or senses. It is attained through spiritual practice and the grace of God or the spiritual master.

Jnana Yoga – 'Union through the path of knowledge.' The spiritual path of supreme knowledge, which entails insight and understanding of the true nature of the Self and of the world. This involves a deep, sincere study of the scriptures, detachment (vairagya), discrimination (viveka), meditation, and the intellectual method of self-inquiry – "who/what am 'I'?" and "I am Brahman" – which is used to break through the illusion of maya and attain the state of Self-realization.

Kali – 'The Dark One.' A form of the Divine Mother. ('Dark' in this context refers to her boundlessness, and the fact that she is unknowable and incomprehensible to the very limited range of the mind and intellect.) From the viewpoint of the ego, she may seem frightening because she destroys the ego. But she destroys the ego and transforms us only out of her immeasurable compassion. Kali has many forms; in her benevolent form, she is known as Bhadra Kali. A devotee knows that behind her fierce façade, the loving Mother is to be found, protecting her children and bestowing the grace of enlightenment.

Kalidas – (About 400 ce) India's greatest Sanskrit poet and dramatist. Author of Meghduta, Raguvamsa, Sakuntala, etc.

Kama – Lust.

Karma – Action, deed.

Karma Yoga – 'Union through action.' The spiritual path of detached, selfless service and of dedicating the fruit of all of one's actions to God.

Krishna – 'He who draws us to himself'; 'the Dark One.' ('Dark' in this context refers to his boundlessness, and the fact that he is unknowable and incomprehensible to the very limited range of the mind and intellect.) He was born into a royal family, but grew up with foster parents and lived as a young cowherd in Vrindavan, where he was loved and worshipped by his devoted companions, the gopis (milkmaids and cowherd girls) and gopas (cowherd boys). Krishna later became the ruler of Dwaraka. He was a friend of and adviser to his cousins, the Pandavas, especially Arjuna, to whom he revealed his teachings – see Bhagavad Gita.

Kriya Yoga – A part of traditional tantric practices – mostly breathing exercises.

Kundalini – 'The Serpent Power.' The spiritual energy that rests like a coiled snake at the base of the spine. Through spiritual practice it is made to rise through the sushumna canal, a subtle nerve within the spine, and to move up through the chakras (energy centers). As the kundalini rises from one chakra to the next, the spiritual aspirant begins to experience finer, more subtle levels of consciousness. The kundalini finally reaches the highest chakra at the top of the head, the sahasrara. This process of the awakening of kundalini leads to Self-realization.

Laya Yoga – 'Union through dissolution or absorption.' Based on the development of the chakras and on awakening kundalini energy. A yoga though which the aspirant's lower nature dissolves and one is awakened to bliss and the transcendental consciousness.

Linga – 'Symbol', 'defining sign.' The principle of creativity; often worshipped as a symbol of Lord Shiva. A Shiva linga is generally an elongated oval stone.

Mahabharata – One of the two great Indian historical epics, the other being the Ramayana. It is a great treatise on dharma and spirituality. The story deals mainly with the conflict between the Pandavas and the Kauravas and the great war at Kurukshetra. Containing 100,000 verses, it is the longest epic poem in the world. It was written about 3,200 bce by the sage Vyasa.

Mahatma – 'Great soul.' When Amma uses the word mahatma, she is referring to a Self-realized soul.

Mantra – Sacred formula or prayer, which is constantly repeated. This awakens one's dormant spiritual power and helps one to reach the ultimate goal. It is most effective if received from a realized spiritual master during initiation. A mantra is integrally connected to the reality which it represents, being that reality in its 'seed' form. The mantra, or 'seed,' within the aspirant is nourished by being constantly repeated with concentration, until it finally germinates into the experience of the Supreme Reality.

Matham – Religion.

Maya – Illusion; the divine power or veil with which God, in the divine play of Creation, conceals Himself and gives the impression of the many, thereby creating the illusion of separation. As maya veils Reality, it deludes us, making us believe that true perfection is to be found outside ourselves.

Moksha – Final spiritual liberation.

Mudra – A physical gesture or posture, usually expressed with the hands, containing deep spiritual meaning.

Muruga – 'Beautiful One.' Also known as Subramanya, Muruga is a god created by Shiva to assist souls in their evolution, especially through the practice of yoga. He is the brother of Ganesha.

Nadi Shastra – Nadi = conduit. A particular branch of predictive astrology, e.g., Agastya Nadi

Nadopasana – Devotion and worship through music

Narasimha – The Divine Man-Lion; a partial incarnation of Vishnu.

Narayana – Nara = knowledge, water. 'He who is established in supreme knowledge'; 'He who dwells in the causal waters.' A name of Vishnu.

Natya Shastra – The science of dance, music, and drama.

Parvati – 'Daughter of the mountain.' Shiva's divine consort; a name of the Goddess, the Divine Mother.

Payasam – A sweet rice dish.

Prakriti – Primordial nature; the material principle of the world which, in association with Purusha, creates the universe; the basic matter of which the universe consists.

Prasad(am)– Consecrated offering or gift from a holy person or temple, often in the form of food.

Puja – 'Adoration.' Sacred ritual; ceremonial worship.

Purana – The Puranas are epic stories depicting the lives of the gods, through which the four objectives of humanity (purusharthas) – righteous living (dharma), wealth (artha), desire (kama) and liberation (moksha) – are propounded.

Purusha – The consciousness that dwells within the body; the pure, unblemished Universal Consciousness/Existence.

Raja Yoga – The path of meditation.

Rama – 'Giver of Joy.' The divine hero in the epic Ramayana. He was an incarnation of Lord Vishnu, and is considered to be the ideal of dharma and virtue.

Ramayana – 'The life of Rama.' One of India's two great Indian historical epics (the other being the Mahabharata), depicting the life of Rama, written by Valmiki. Rama was an incarnation of Vishnu. A major part of the epic describes how Sita, Rama's wife, was abducted and taken to Sri Lanka by Ravana, the demon king, and how she was rescued by Rama and his devotees, including his great devotee Hanuman.

Rishi – Rsi = to know. Self-realized seer. Usually refers to the seven Rishis of ancient India, i.e., Self-realized souls who could 'see' the Supreme Truth.

Samskara – Samskara has two meanings: the totality of impressions imprinted on the mind by experiences from this or previous lives, which influence the life of a human being – his or her nature, actions, state of mind, etc.; the kindling of the right understanding (knowledge) within each person, leading to the refinement of his or her character.

Sanatana Dharma – The Eternal Religion; the Eternal Principle. The traditional name for Hinduism.

Saraswati – The Goddess of Learning.

Satya – Truth.

Satya Yuga – The Age of Truth (satya); also called Krita Yuga. There is a cycle of four ages or time periods in creation (see yuga in glossary). The Satya Yuga is the age when goodness and truth prevail everywhere, and every manifestation or activity is close to the purest ideal. It is sometimes referred to as the Golden Age.

Shakti – Power; a name of the Universal Mother, the dynamic aspect of Brahman.

Shankaracharya – (788 – 820 ce) A great philosopher who revived and revitalized the Hindu religion. Founder of the Advaita School, which declares that only Brahman is real, all else is false.

Shastra – Science or specialized knowledge.

Shiva – 'The Auspicious One'; 'the Gracious One'; 'the Good One.' A form of the Supreme Being. The masculine Principle; Consciousness. Also, the aspect of the Trinity associated with the dissolution of the universe, the destruction of that which ultimately is not real.

Shiva linga – A linga symbolizing Shiva. (see linga)

Svara Yoga – The path of using breathing exercises to attain Self-realization.

Tantra – A traditional system of spiritual practices which enables the practitioner in the midst of worldly activities to realize that the joy experienced in objects actually arises from within.

Tapas – 'Heat.' Self-discipline, austerities, penance, and self-sacrifice; spiritual practices which burn up the impurities of the mind.

The three worlds – Heaven, earth, and the netherworld; the three states of consciousness.

Upadhi – Limiting adjunct, e.g., name, form, attribute; instrument; tool.

Upanishad – 'To sit at the feet of the Master'; 'that which destroys ignorance.' The Upanishads are the fourth and concluding portions of the Vedas. They expound the philosophy known as Vedanta.

Vairagi – 'The detached one' (refers to Shiva).

Vairagya – Detachment, dispassion.

Valmiki – A robber who became a great saint after realizing how mistaken his values and assumptions were, and after undertaking rigorous spiritual practices under the guidance of the Rishis. He is a great example of how it is possible to completely die to the past, no matter how negative one's actions may have been.

Vastu – 'Nature'; 'environment.' The ancient Vedic science of architecture, containing complex principles and practices for the construction of buildings in harmonious balance with nature and the universe.

Vedanta – 'Veda conclusion.' The philosophy of the Upanishads, the concluding part of the Vedas, which holds the Ultimate Truth to be 'One without a second.'

Vedas – 'Knowledge, wisdom.' The ancient, sacred scriptures of Hinduism. A collection of holy texts in Sanskrit, which are divided into four parts: Rig, Yajur, Sama and Atharva. The Vedas, which are among the world's oldest scriptures, consist of 100,000 verses, as well as additional prose. They were brought into the world by the Rishis, who were Self-realized sages. The Vedas are considered to be the direct revelation of the Supreme Truth.

Vishnu – 'The All-Pervading.' A name of God. He is usually worshipped in the form of two of his incarnations, Krishna and Rama.

Viveka – Discrimination; the ability to discriminate between the Real and the unreal, between the eternal and the transient, dharma and adharma (unrighteousness), etc.

Yaga yajnas – Elaborate Vedic sacrificial rite.

Yajna – Offering.

Yoga – 'To unite.' Union with the Supreme Being; a broad term that refers to the various practical methods through which one can attain oneness with the Divine; a path that leads to Self-realization.

Yuga – Age or eon. There are four yugas: the Satya or Krita Yuga (the Golden Age), Treta Yuga, Dwapara Yuga, and Kali Yuga (the Dark Age). We are presently living in the Kali Yuga. The yugas are said to succeed each other almost endlessly.

www.ingramcontent.com/pod-product-compliance
Lightning Source LLC
Chambersburg PA
CBHW070614050426
42450CB00011B/3057